Life at the Edge of the Wave

Lessons from the Community College

MARGUERITE M. CULP AND STEVEN R. HELFGOT
Compiling Editors

National Association of Student
Personnel Administrators, Inc.

Library of Congress
Cataloging-in-Publication Data
Life at the edge of the wave : lessons from the community college /
Marguerite M. Culp and Steven R. Helfgot, editors.
    p.   cm.
    ISBN 0-931654-24-6
1. Community colleges--United States. 2. Community college students --
Services for--United States. 3. Student affairs services--United States. 4.
Educational sociology--United States. I. Culp, Marguerite McGann. II.
Helfgot, Steven R.
LB2328.15.U62L54   1998   98-14234
378.1'543'0973--dc21   CIP

Monograph Series Editorial Board
1998

Patrick Love, *editor*
Kent State University
Kent, Ohio

Other NASPA Monograph Titles

A Student Affairs Guide to the ADA and Disability Issues

Advice from the Dean: A Personal Perspective on the Philosophy, Roles, and Approaches of a Dean at a Small Liberal Arts College

Different Voices: Gender and Perspective in Student Affairs Administration

Diversity, Disunity, and Campus Community

From Survival to Success: Promoting Minority Student Retention

Puzzles and Pieces in Wonderland: The Promise and Practice of Student Affairs Research

Student Affairs and Campus Dissent: Reflection of the Past and Challenge for the Future

The Invisible Leaders: Student Affairs Mid-Managers

The New Professional: A Resource Guide for New Student Affairs Professionals and Their Supervisors

The Role of Student Affairs in Institution-Wide Enrollment Management Strategies

Working with International Students and Scholars on American Campuses

NASPA's monographs may be purchased by contacting NASPA at 1875 Connecticut Avenue, NW, Suite 418, Washington, D.C. 20009-5728; 202-265-7500 (tel) or 202-797-1157 (fax).

CONTENTS

v

Chapter Six, cont'd.

Introduction

———— ◆ ————

by Steven R. Helfgot

nyone who has taken a graduate course in the history of American higher education has heard the story. That history, over the last 200 plus years, has been one of growing egalitarianism and increased access. Our earliest universities were for the elite: those with talent, those with time, those with sufficient funds, those who came from the right families. Decades later, the opening of land grant colleges — public universities in today's parlance — made higher education available to those who were not members of the elite, to the public. While these colleges, over the years, opened higher education to millions, a certain elitism of ability, a meritocracy, still characterizes many of them. Certainly, at the flagship public universities across the country, admission is selective, often on par with that of the elite private institutions. The University of California, for example, is mandated by law to admit the top 12.5 percent of graduating high school seniors from across the state.

A continuous tension seems to exist between the impulse for egalitarianism on the one hand and, on the other, the belief that a college education is somehow to be reserved for the best and the brightest. So, while we reserve the so-called first tier public universities for the academic elite, our egalitarian impulses are at least somewhat satisfied because, theoretically, these universities are accessible to those who are intellectually able but lacking the means to pay the cost of the elite private institutions. Still, we are not completely satisfied. A college education has been made available to those who most deserve it but what about everybody else, the 80 percent or more of high school graduates who cannot qualify for admission to the elite private universities and the flagship state universities?

Again, we all know the answer. From coast to coast, there are roughly 2,000 other institutions, both public and private, that provide a college education to the vast majority of students, those whose abilities fall nearest the center of the bell-shaped curve or those who have not yet lived up to their potential. These are the schools that welcomed veterans with GI benefits after World War II, Korea, and Viet Nam and that were flooded by baby-boomers in the 1960s and 1970s. For several decades — perhaps even until today — these colleges and universities have in many ways resembled their more elite cousins: different, perhaps, but not so different that anyone would question the family resemblance. Their students, mostly but not exclusively white and from the vast American middle class, placed in the second and even the third quarters of their high school graduating classes. Some were commuters but most were on residential campuses, living in residence halls, Greek houses, and in off-campus apartments. Some were the children of college graduates; many were first-generation college students. They were upwardly mobile, on their way to careers as teachers and social workers, as MBAs and CPAs. Some were preparing for law school, even for medical school, and some would get hooked on the academic life and pursue graduate study.

For most of us working in the student affairs profession today, these were and are our students. They were the ones we learned about in graduate school and the ones with whom most of us have worked, be it for five or twenty-five years. They are the students that allow us to share a more or less common language and to engage in meaningful discourse with one another. For while the Ivy League school, the flagship state university, the small liberal arts college, and the obscure state college may differ from each other in several ways, their students would, by and large, still fit our image of *the college student*, who is described in our developmental theories and to whom we apply those theories.

In the aftermath of the 1960s, though, things changed. For all our egalitarianism, for all our desire to bring higher education to the masses, these masses were still somewhat narrowly defined. Ethnic minorities, women, adults, and those who previously had not been thought of as "college material" were, for the most part, not included. Only in the wake of the 1960s' social protest movements — for civil rights and women's rights most notably — did these new groups begin to enter higher education. Colleges and universities, however, were already bursting at the seams with the baby-boomers, and these new students, many argued, were not really well prepared for college, and many of those who were prepared could not afford to go. Where would they go? How would they enter the higher education mainstream? The answer, it seemed, was that they would go to the junior college along with the boomers for whom there was not sufficient space on four-year college and university campuses.

Junior colleges had been in existence — in relatively small numbers — for decades. The major purpose of two-year institutions had always been to prepare students for and, at the end of the sophomore year, transfer them to senior or four-year colleges and universities. Some, as part of their mission, prepared students for certain skilled careers (nursing, for example) that did not require a baccalaureate degree. Starting in the mid-1960s, though, and continuing to this day, junior colleges — reconfigured as *community colleges* because they were geographically located in a particular community, governed by a locally elected or appointed board of trustees, supported by local property taxes, and mandated to serve students from a local district — became the point of first contact with higher education for so-called new students. For more than a decade, starting in the late-1960s, new community colleges opened across the United States at a rate that would have put McDonalds or Wal-Mart to shame, until more than 1,500 had been established.

Today, these community colleges have student bodies that range in size from several hundred to 30,000 or more. Many of the more than 6 million students they enroll are from the new populations and, in many cases, most of their students are from those populations. Some may also have large numbers of traditional students but others have almost none. With the growth and expansion of community colleges in the last quarter-century, our national egalitarian impulse has truly taken hold and higher education, not without ongoing debate, has become a right rather than a privilege. As the enrollment figures demonstrate, anyone and everyone can have access to higher education through their local community college.

For those of us in student affairs work and for our instructional colleagues as well, the nature of our work and clientele has dramatically changed. New students come to our campuses in waves, and while the students in each wave are new to higher education, that may be the only characteristic they share. Adult women were and are part of a wave of new students; they are very different from the wave that includes recent immigrants who are not native speakers of English. Both are, in turn, different from the wave of middle-aged men who have been downsized out of what they thought were lifelong careers. All of these groups are different from the continuing wave of the *unders* — the underprepared, the under-represented, the underachieving, the underclass. All, however, encounter the world of higher education in the community college. That is where they start; it is not, however, where many of them finish. Many transfer to senior institutions to complete an undergraduate degree, often seeking an urban commuter institution that accommodates them in much the same way as the community college. Indeed, the students who attend community colleges and urban commuter institutions account for a majority of American college students. Increasingly, however, they are starting to find their way to more traditional colleges and universities. And it is that fact, more than anything else, that gives purpose to this volume and to the desire for those of us in two-year institutions to share our perspective with our colleagues in four-year schools.

Our students and, increasingly, *your* students represent the majority of American students, but they are in many ways disenfranchised by the student affairs profession. Looking at our theory, our conference programs, our research, our literature, and our graduate preparation programs, one would have to conclude that the majority of college students are still 18- to 22-year olds attending four-year institutions on a full-time basis while living on campus. One would further have to conclude that most practitioners in the field work in such institutions and also that most of the future jobs in the field will be in them, but these conclusions are no longer accurate: indeed, the vast majority of our professional knowledge is about a minority of our students.

For example, Astin's (1984) Involvement Theory has received overwhelming support in the profession since its introduction. At its core is a notion that is both reasonable and powerful: the more involved students are in their education, the more time and energy they give to activities related to their educational goals, the more successful they will be. This makes perfect sense, and so student affairs administrators have made substantial efforts to increase opportunities for students to be more involved. From study groups to on-campus jobs, to out-of-class contacts with faculty, to club affiliations, we have stimulated and encouraged student involvement.

This involvement does not make sense to the new community college student, however, or even to the more traditional community college student. If these students were to look at the involvement theory, they might conclude that because they do not see themselves in the theory they are doomed to fail as college students. The theory seems to presuppose that college students attend school full time, live on campus, and have no significant non-college related obligations that demand time and attention (perhaps even more time and attention than does school). In this theory, college is the focus of the students' lives, with time and energy of course available for the increased involvement that will lead to success.

Because community college students do not fit the theory's assumptions about college students, they cannot, by application of the theory, do what is needed to be successful. They do not have the time for involvement because they are working full time and have family and sometimes community responsibilities that demand a greater priority than school. These students are — of necessity — what I have called elsewhere, "educational surfers" (Helfgot, 1997, p. 4). They skim across the wave of higher education, desperately trying to keep their balance, hoping not to fall off their board before arriving at the distant shore that is the end of the ride, a degree. They will not, cannot, jump off the board for a leisurely swim nor can they linger on the beach. They have other things to do; they need to move on. These community college students are successful *despite* what the theory would suggest. Involvement theory itself neither explicitly nor implicitly acknowledges their existence because they do not fit the model. Most disconcerting is that although the theory excludes community college students and the many students in urban commuter institutions who have similar characteristics, its proponents do not recognize that it is applicable to only part of the college student population. The theory purports to be applicable to *all* college students.

This is but one example among many. Research on college students tends to be conducted by research professors, and research professors are found in senior institutions. The subjects of their studies are often the students in their own institutions, and these students are, more often than not, traditional students. As more students from community colleges arrive on the university campus, they become available for research and study, and from this research, theory is beginning to emerge that acknowledges nontraditional students. Some writings about nontraditional students (nontraditional on the four-year campus, that is, but very much traditional at community colleges) are now appearing, and that is all well and good, but theory takes time to work its way into the field and even more time to be translated into practice. While this process evolves, however, the needs of the new students are not being met, not because of ill will or incompetence but merely as a result of ignorance. Student affairs administrators employ the models they have learned and apply the training they have received, as they should, but neither is appropriate to these students.

Community college student affairs practitioners have, however, worked with these students for years, and even though we may not have developed theoretical models that interpret them, we have developed a broad, deep, and clear understanding of who they are, what they need, and how we might best meet their needs. From that understanding have come practical models and even more practical and useful programs, services, and approaches for working with these students.

The purpose of this monograph is to share practical knowledge about new students generally and about specific groups of new students in particular in order to elucidate at least a few common themes or underlying approaches for dealing with new students, whoever they may be. Merely describing the wave or waves of new students currently making their way into the campuses of four-year institutions is insufficient. Behind them will be the next wave, and the next, and the next. That is what we have come to expect in community college student affairs work, and we practice our craft and live our professional lives in terms of the leading edge of the current wave of new students. Indeed, even as we write these words, those responsible for student services at hundreds of community colleges across the country are planning for the newest wave, the tens of thousands of new students who will be making their way to community college campuses as a result of welfare reform legislation. Who will they be? What unique needs will they have? What new services or approaches will meet those needs? Soon they will begin to arrive and then we will know. And that information, too, will in time be passed on. For now, though, we can offer what we have learned from those waves of students who have already passed through our institutions. The assumption at the core of this monograph is that the professional lives of student affairs practitioners in many colleges and universities will, sooner or later, come to closely resemble those of their community college colleagues.

In Chapter One, Marguerite M. Culp describes the current reality in community colleges, a reality "at the edge of the wave." She details the multiple challenges facing community colleges, many of which will soon face four-year institutions as well. She enumerates the various functions of two-year college student affairs divisions and compares and contrasts them to similar functional areas in four-year institutions. In conclusion, she offers some projections for the future that student services administrators in both two- and four-year colleges will be able to use to organize professional practice.

In an environment like the community college, which is characterized by change, the need to organize professional practice is very real. Without some consistent organizing principle, the need to respond to continual change could reduce a student affairs organization to chaos. Student affairs divisions in community colleges do change in response to their changing environment, but a consistent organizing principle from year to year, and even from decade to decade, has been a focus on student success. In Chapter Two, I illustrate this focus by describing a Student Success Imperative and contrasting it with the American College Personnel Association's (ACPA) recent *Student Learning Imperative.* More than simply describing the elements of a student services program focused on student success, this chapter also serves to highlight, once again, how some of our major professional initiatives seem oblivious to the fact that large numbers of students are not at all like traditional college students. Yet, much of our theory and literature, like the *Student Learning Imperative*, seems to ignore this fact.

For this reason and others, theory, developmental theory in particular, has always provided something of a dilemma for two-year college student services staff members. On the one hand, community colleges are inherently developmental institutions — development of everything, from basic academic skills to self-esteem to a core sense of identity, is an integral part of working with community college students, making theory very appealing. On the other hand, much of our theory has been based on student populations completely unlike those in the two-year college, making the theory somewhat suspect. In recent years, the profession as a whole and its theoreticians in particular have begun, albeit very slowly, to recognize the need to include new students in our formulations. Newer, more inclusive theories have begun to emerge and older theories have been revised. In Chapter Three, Linda Reisser, who worked with Arthur Chickering in the revision of his theory, examines the role of theory in working with nontraditional students. She then offers examples of how theory translates into everyday practice and concludes by suggesting priorities for the future, most notably the need for research.

Community colleges are intimate institutions, where less division exists between functional areas than in many colleges and universities. Everyone is involved in everyone else's business. Student affairs and academic affairs are, for example, intimately connected. In Chapter Four, Marguerite M. Culp discusses this relationship and the ways in which student services administrators can "infiltrate academe" to enhance opportunities for student success and also for faculty and staff member success.

In Chapter Five, Jack and Janna Becherer make the theoretical discussions of the previous chapters more concrete as they offer examples of successful community college programs. The several programs and services they describe illustrate some of the ways in which community colleges work effectively and creatively with diverse students and diverse needs.

Chapter Six, the concluding chapter, offers a series of short essays on the tools that will be required for successful student affairs practice into the new century. In the first essay of this chapter, I suggest that to meet student needs effectively we must think about the students in new ways.

Community college student services administrators think of professional preparation as a tool. Good preparation programs result in the development of a competent staff that can accomplish the demanding and constantly changing jobs in community college student affairs work. The problem has been that too many preparation programs have not been sufficiently aware of the unique needs of community colleges. Cynthia Johnson offers her suggestions for a graduate program that would take into account the needs of community colleges, and by extension, the emerging needs of four-year institutions.

Technology is perhaps the ultimate tool for tomorrow. As technological tools become ubiquitous on both two- and four-year campuses, both opportunities and dangers are presented. In the third of our essays, Michael Rooney shares lessons about implementing new computer systems that he learned while visiting several schools during a sabbatical leave. The need for being focused on students and the importance of involving the whole campus community in developing the technology agenda are among the most important lessons he imparts.

Our student affairs divisions have an organizational structure with different staff members occupying various positions; those are things we take for granted. Marguerite M. Culp cautions us not to take them for granted. How we organize the staff members we employ, and the professional roles we have them fill all make a difference. Organization and staffing, done well and wisely, can be a tool for our success and that of our students. Done poorly, they can hinder us and hurt our efforts to help students be successful.

Beyond professional preparation and intelligent organization and staffing, there is a need to help staff members remain current, both in the dynamic and rapidly changing community college and increasingly in the four-year college environment. Marie Nock, in the fifth of this chapter's essays, shares her insights and suggestions about effective staff development programs.

The themes of partnership and collaboration run through this monograph. Much as we need to re-envision the way we look at students, however, we also need to re-envision the way we look at partnerships, especially in the area of student transfer, the axis on which the relationship between two-year and four-year colleges revolves. In the final essay, Erlinda Martinez and Bill Scroggins remind us that the most powerful tool we have may well be our ability to think in an innovative and creative manner, and they challenge us to use this tool to further the best interests of students.

Finally, it is important to note that we all have taken on this task with a mixture of excitement and trepidation. We are excited that NASPA has embraced the notion that there is something happening in the community college that is important to the profession *as a whole*. Our fear is that our message will be misunderstood. Our insights, the information we have to share, perhaps even the advice we might offer, does not come from some sense of knowing more or being in a superior position. Rather, it comes from knowing that our institutions, for whatever reason, and for better or for worse, have been placed at the leading edge of the wave. And from that position we are perhaps able to gain the first glimpse of what is coming. We share this information out of an ongoing sense of commitment to our students and in a spirit of collegiality with all those who work on their behalf in both two and four-year institutions. Our hope is that the more we all know, the better that we can all do . . . for students, for our institutions, and for our profession.

References

Astin, A. (1984). Student involvement: A developmental theory for higher education. *Journal of College Student Development, 25*, 297-308.

Helfgot, S. R. (1997). Learning communities: Are we wearing professional blinders? *The Commuter, 22*, 4-5.

CHAPTER ONE

Our Present, Your Future

by Marguerite M. Culp

ny community college practitioner who visits an urban public college or university that serves commuter students feels at home immediately. Over the past decade, such institutions have come to resemble community colleges in terms of the students they serve, the challenges they face, and the strategies they use to meet these challenges. In fact, faculty and staff members from these institutions recognize instantly that the problems community colleges tried to resolve in the past decade are problems that urban public institutions face today. Suburban and rural colleges and universities are beginning to experience a student population shift as they enroll more community college transfer students, respond to state mandates to serve students from populations historically under-represented on their campuses, and expand their target audiences in response to enrollment management initiatives. The wave has not yet reached faculty and staff members from highly selective state and private institutions, partly because the number of students from under-represented populations has not reached a critical mass on their campuses but also because of the perception that these institutions are inhospitable to at-risk students.

When the Wave Hits

As soon as the number of students from under-represented populations reaches a critical mass, many institutions experience culture shock. Usually the first ones in their families to pursue a four-year degree, these students have no guides or coaches at home, no one to help them navigate a system that is often set up for the convenience of the faculty and staff rather than the convenience of the students. Many of these students have complex personal and educational needs that the institution is unable to identify much less meet, and they do not learn the way earlier students have learned, i.e., by listening to lectures and taking notes. To add to the challenge, a small percentage are underprepared and unmotivated, even though they have earned a two-year degree or met the institution's admissions requirements. The institution's first response is to try to fit these students into existing conceptual models and programs. The result is predictable: escalating drop-out rates, faculty longing for the "good old days," pressure to change admissions standards, and community questions about the institution's effectiveness. When the institution realizes that the students will not (or cannot) fit into the existing structure, it tries to adjust programs, people, and services. Experimenting with minor adjustments rather than instituting program transformations fails to meet the challenge, further erodes faculty and staff morale, and usually culminates in organizational paralysis — and the placing of blame in all the wrong places.

Surviving the Wave

The population group from which colleges and universities draw their students is changing. Since the applicant pool increasingly resembles the pool from which community colleges have drawn their students for the last two decades, it stands to reason that colleges and universities can profit from studying community colleges, building on their successes, and learning from their mistakes — and that community colleges and the students they serve can benefit from building partnerships with their college and university colleagues.

Subsequent chapters in this monograph will discuss specific community college practices, programs, and strategies in student affairs. Since the health of these programs is generally related to the health of the institution in which they exist, it is helpful to look at the characteristics that distinguish thriving community colleges from barely surviving ones. These characteristics offer a starting point for thinking about what colleges and universities can learn from their community college colleagues and provide a conceptual framework for the rest of this chapter. Community colleges that are most agile at riding the wave and meeting the needs of students from under-represented populations are those whose faculty, staff members, and board members learn how to:

- Create, communicate, and live by a shared vision.
- Scan the environment to predict the characteristics and needs of the next student wave.

- Focus on learning and student success.
- Redefine and reward effective teaching.
- Emphasize outcomes rather than seat time.
- Create new theories to help faculty and staff members understand and meet the needs of the students who are now in their classes, not students from years past.
- Allocate resources to help faculty and staff members update their skills.
- Provide faculty and staff members with tomorrow's tools, particularly in the area of technology.
- Redesign student support services.
- Create community partnerships that increase the quality of high school graduates and community college transfer students, connect the classroom to the real world, and blur the line between the college and its consumers.

LIFE AT THE EDGE OF THE WAVE

To understand how community college student affairs administrators acquired their expertise in dealing with students from populations historically under-represented in higher education, colleagues in colleges and universities need to understand the community college: its mission and goals, the students it serves, the faculty who staff it, and the challenges it has faced in its brief history.

The Institution

According to the *Chronicle of Higher Education Almanac* (1997), 14 community colleges enrolled over 22,000 students in the fall of 1995. That same year, three of the top ten colleges in terms of size were community colleges, and 15 percent of the largest educational institutions in the country were public two-year colleges. The 14 largest community colleges were multi-campus operations serving urban areas in fairly large states: Arizona, California, Florida, Ohio, Oregon, Virginia, and Texas. The 14 smallest community colleges served rural residents in communities throughout the country. Between the 14 largest and the 14 smallest community colleges were 1,019 public and 415 private two-year institutions that enrolled 5,492,529 students in the fall of 1995 and awarded 539,691 associate degrees during the 1994-95 academic year.

In its *National Profile of Community Colleges: Trends and Statistics* (Phillippe, 1995), the American Association of Community Colleges concluded that two-year colleges were responsible for 76 percent of the net increase in higher education enrollments in this decade. The mission of most community colleges, however, extends far beyond preparing students to transfer. Community colleges offer a vast array of services to their communities — often in partnership with business, civic, and educational groups — that include two-year degrees and one-year certificates, courses to help mature workers upgrade their skills, workplace literacy and workforce training programs, developmental education classes for underprepared students, and targeted activities to meet specific community needs. And community colleges offer these services at a reasonable cost: the average community college student pays $1,245 in tuition and fees versus $2,848 for students in public colleges and universities and $12,239 for students in private institutions (*Chronicle Almanac*, 1997).

The Students
Whatever their size and wherever their location, public two-year colleges provide access to higher education to a broad spectrum of the community. Between 1965 and 1992, the percentage of students who entered higher education through the community college increased from 20 percent to 38 percent, while the percentage of first-time college first-year students attending a community college increased from 24 percent to 49 percent (Phillippe, 1995). As Figure 1 demonstrates, public community colleges provide access to higher education for an increasing number of students from under-represented populations.

Figure 1
Public Two-Year College Enrollment by Ethnic Group

Ethnic Group	1976	1980	1990	1995
African American	409,500	437,900	481,400	588,200
Asian American	78,200	122,500	210,300	308,700
International	39,200	60,300	63,600	85,600
Latino/a	207,500	249,800	408,900	590,300
Native American	39,300	45,200	52,400	63,000
White	2,974,300	3,413,100	3,779,800	3,642,100

Community colleges also made education more accessible to students with disabilities. More than half of all college students with a reported disability attend two-year institutions; in fact, students with disabilities make up 8 percent of the community college population (Phillippe, 1995).

Describing the typical community college student presents a real challenge. A *National Profile of Community Colleges: Trends and Statistics,* prepared for the American Association of Community Colleges (Phillippe, 1995), examined headcount enrollment for the fall 1992 term and offered seven observations about community college students.

- 58 percent were female.
- 27 percent defined themselves as members of an ethnic or minority group.
- The average age was 29, and 33 percent were over 30.
- Over 65 percent attended part time.
- Over 65 percent were employed, 36 percent full time and 29 percent part time.
- Many are the first in their family to attend college.
- Most have significant family and job responsibilities.

Though the themes suggested by the data have proven to be fairly accurate over time, community colleges serve a fluid student population whose demographics change from term to term. Single semester figures offer a snapshot of community college enrollments at a specific time and help student affairs administrators identify the different on- and off-campus support systems that a current semester's students need in order to succeed in college. Interpreted correctly, such figures would allow colleges and universities to anticipate the needs of the transfer students they will be serving in the following two years.

The Faculty

Campus literature is very clear about the mission of community colleges in America: they are *teaching institutions* with faculty who pride themselves on being teachers first. Community college faculty, however, pay a price for their dedication to teaching. The average pay for full-time community college faculty members in 1995-96 was $43,295, while their counterparts at public universities earned $55,068 (*Chronicle Almanac*, 1997). Preliminary data from the National Study of Student Learning indicate that this dedication to teaching pays off for students. When background characteristics are taken into account, "students at community colleges made first-year changes in reading comprehension, mathematics, and critical thinking that were generally indistinguishable in magnitude from those made by students in four-year colleges" (Pascarella, Edison, Nora, Hagedorn & Terenzini, 1995-96, p. 36).

In a study published in 1990, Baker, Roueche, and Gillett-Karam identified six characteristics of exemplary community college instructors.

- They are student-centered teachers who emphasize active learning and view themselves as facilitators rather than information transmitters.
- They understand that adult learners are unique and need hands-on learning.
- They employ strategies that keep students involved in the learning process.
- They lead in the classroom using all of the motivational, cognitive, and interpersonal skills at their disposal.
- They understand students' needs, concerns, and interests and integrate them into the teaching-learning process.
- They value learning in the broad sense, and they continually look for and reward new perspectives and new possibilities.

Although all community college teachers are not exemplary, the bottom line is that most community college faculty value teaching, continually search for more effective ways to help students learn, and struggle to reach all students, not just those able to teach themselves.

The Challenges

For several decades, community college faculty and staff members have successfully responded to internal and external threats. An examination of how community colleges turned most of these threats into opportunities is essential to understanding the American community college.

Competing Visions. Supporters and critics have yet to agree on a national community college vision. Most community college leaders refused to wait for a national definition; they worked with the faculty, staff, and community to create their own focus, sense of purpose, and unifying vision and used these as yardsticks to make and measure the impact of decisions. Given the diversity of the communities they serve and the speed with which they must respond to community needs, the consensus is that community colleges must operate more on local visions than a single national vision.

Changing Student Demographics. Community college students did not just look different from one year to the next, they *were* different in fundamental ways — ways that made measuring, understanding, and responding to them difficult. Many were undermotivated, underprepared, and over-committed *by necessity* to a life outside the college. Most were dealing with life and learning transitions — some planned and pleasant, most unexpected and unsettling. These students needed support, in and out of the classroom, in order to succeed, but the type of support they needed varied from year to year, if not from term to term. To meet these challenges, community colleges developed data gathering strategies to identify at-risk students early in their academic lives, extensive on- and off-campus support programs, and computer-based student tracking and early warning systems. They also learned to eliminate, restructure, or add programs quickly and efficiently.

Changing Faculty Demographics. Many community college founding faculty retired or planned to retire in the 1990s. Although these retirements provide opportunities to attract new and innovative faculty, they also have the potential to strip institutions of their history and of the senior faculty members who view their commitment to the community college as part of a calling rather than just a job. Anticipating the changing of the guard, community colleges defined their vision for the future and clearly articulated their expectations to candidates, screening committees, and the hiring managers. In some states, such as Florida, community college presidents worked with colleagues in the state university system to develop graduate programs capable of producing community college faculty members with the skills needed to teach tomorrow's students.

Multiple Overlapping Constituencies. From their inception, community colleges struggled to meet the needs of many different types of students and deal with the constituencies that either represented these various students or hoped to benefit from their educational experiences. Area high schools, colleges and universities, community agencies, businesses, advocacy groups, state and federal government offices, and civic leaders viewed themselves as stakeholders in the local community college. As stakeholders, they wanted their needs met, their wants considered, and their values upheld, if not enshrined. But the needs, wants, and values of one group of stakeholders often conflicted with the needs, wants, and values of another, equally influential group. Community colleges learned that shared vision and strong leadership at the top were the only way to avoid becoming victims of multiple overlapping constituencies. They also learned that everyone — presidents, administrators, faculty, staff members, and even students — had to be active in the community, committed to creating partnerships, and constantly involved in educating stakeholders about their rights and responsibilities in the educational process.

Reliance on Part-time Faculty. The American Association of Community Colleges believes that part-time faculty outnumber full-time faculty now at most community colleges by a two-to-one margin (Phillippe, 1995).

Because of faculty workloads, however, the largest percentage of sections are still taught by full-time professors. Community colleges believed that the use of adjunct faculty exposed students to professionals who were up-to-date in their fields, provided students and full-time faculty with valuable off-campus contacts, and kept tuition prices low, but this reliance on adjuncts created unique challenges for educational institutions. Community colleges learned that adjunct faculty were successful only when they were mentored, valued, rewarded appropriately, and incorporated in a meaningful way into the life of the college. This was achieved by forming adjunct faculty associations, providing adjuncts with office space, establishing full-time faculty mentors for all adjuncts, having them participate in departmental meetings, and giving them access to travel and training funds, awards, and pay based on years of service and performance ratings.

Structures Designed to Serve Yesterday's Students. During the past decade, faculty and student affairs staff members across the country have struggled to change outdated organizational structures and adapt outmoded learning theories and instructional techniques to meet the needs of students whose skills and competencies are at the lowest levels in American history (Roueche & Roueche, 1993). Recognizing the gap between student needs and the skills of the faculty and staff members, community colleges invested a significant percentage of their resources in staff, program, and organizational development. Florida, for example, required community college presidents to earmark a portion of their budgets for program and staff development.

Tired Preparation Programs and Training Models. Student demographics changed so rapidly that most community colleges, in spite of their efforts to remain on top of the wave, were "probably devoting too much energy to preserving the past and not enough to creating the future" (Alfred & Carter, 1996, p. 10). Part of the reason this occurred was that graduate schools continued to prepare subject-matter specialists whose skills were appropriate for university classrooms and student affairs specialists who trained for careers managing college and university residence halls. Community colleges partially compensated by creating their own staff development programs and by working with colleges and universities to add units on the community college to the curriculum and to offer internships to graduate students. But the inability of graduate schools to produce well-trained faculty and student affairs administrators to staff the nation's community colleges was — and is — a serious threat.

Lack of Status. As Pascarella observed in the January/February 1997 issue of *About Campus*, community colleges "have not received anywhere near the attention they deserve," possibly because of "the rather virulent status hierarchy that exists in our system of post-secondary education" (p. 14). Sensitive to their second-class status, community colleges implemented sophisticated institutional effectiveness models, shared outcome data with university colleagues, and marketed their mission more aggressively and more effectively. Community colleges in Florida worked with the State University System (SUS) to develop a feedback loop that provided community colleges with information by major about the performance of their graduates in the SUS.

Competition. Once upon a time, the competition facing community colleges was confined to the educational arena: colleges, universities, and each other. In the 1990s, competitors from outside of education worked hard to compete with traditional higher education providers. Corporations, temporary agencies, and for-profit organizations competed for students and for their share of the higher education dollar in many states (Alfred & Carter, 1996). Community colleges responded by becoming more streamlined, more responsive to community needs, more cost effective, and more visible in the community.

Increase in Legislative Mandates. As the mood of the public changed and state governments became more conservative, public postsecondary educational institutions were faced with legislative mandates designed to increase their effectiveness and accountability. Florida's experiment with performance-based funding for all of higher education and the K-12 system (Tyree & Hellmich, 1995) coupled with average tuition increases of 47 percent between 1987-88 and 1992-93 (Katsinas, 1994) threatened the community college's open door in that state. The Division of Community Colleges dealt with the challenge by volunteering to implement the funding model on an incremental basis, identify problems, and assist the state to modify the formula.

Limited Resources. Higher education's share of state and local budgets was squeezed by the rising costs of K-12 education, law enforcement, and the correction system, as well as the "rising cost of meeting the demand created by a wave of additional students with an increasing diversity of learning styles, educational goals, and support needs" (Conner, 1997, p. 2). Community college leaders followed the 3Rs — redefining priorities, restructuring programs and services, and reallocating resources — to guide their institutions through the lean years. For example, community college presidents in Florida worked with the Division of Community Colleges to eliminate competition for resources by developing a plan to divide money equitably among the 28 community colleges before the legislature allocated any resources to the community college system, thus reducing competition among institutions and presenting a united front to both the House and the

Senate. Austin Community College in Texas implemented formula-driven staffing and funding patterns for all of its campuses in an attempt to reduce the role of politics and personalities in the resource allocation process. Across the nation, community colleges talked with universities about creating joint-use facilities to contain costs, replace competition with collaboration, and increase the higher education opportunities available to the community.

Changing Economic Realities. The demise of the agricultural and manufacturing jobs that fueled America's economic engine throughout the 20th century altered both the nation's economy and the type of education workers required to remain competitive (Carnevale & Desrochers, 1997). Because of their local base and their relationship with business and industry, community colleges were in a unique position to supply the educated workforce that fueled the economy in the last decades the century. Across America, community colleges worked with business and community leaders to create short- and long-term training programs, some leading to degrees and others to certificates, and to streamline transfer degree requirements. Through distance learning initiatives, community colleges met the educational needs of students who did not live in their service districts, city, state, or country. Creating short-term training programs, streamlining degree requirements, and offering distance learning courses forced community colleges to identify their core values, to allocate resources based on these core values, and to determine which programs and services contribute to their bottom line: student success. More important, community colleges learned not to accede to the demands of employers who wanted graduates with a narrow set of job skills and continued to prepare students to become lifelong learners.

RIDING THE WAVE
Community College Student Affairs Programs

Current Status. Student affairs programs in community colleges are as unique as the institutions they serve. Although the organizational charts for student affairs in two- and four-year institutions (with the exception of residence life) may look the same, the way major offices function on the day-to-day basis is very different. Exploring these differences may help colleges and universities anticipate, adapt to, and meet the needs of the students they must serve in the future.

Admissions. Community colleges are open-door institutions whose admissions offices coordinate recruitment efforts, coach students through the application process, interpret the needs of entering students to the institution and the expectations of the institution to the student, anticipate and help the institution respond to changing student demographics and marketplace trends, and troubleshoot for problems that might discourage students from enrolling. Most community college admissions offices establish relationships with prospective applicants and their families long before they are eligible to enter college, sometimes as early as middle school. Two-year college admissions staff members also create partnerships with business and civic groups to generate students for their institutions, and with local high schools in an effort to increase the likelihood that students will be prepared for their college-level classes. In many community colleges, the members of the admissions staff roam the college's service area with laptops and modems, helping students complete the application process on the spot, whether in a high school cafeteria, a mall, a job site, or the workforce development office.

Advising and Educational Planning. Some community colleges rely on faculty advisors, while others hire academic advisors or counselors, and a few share the responsibilities, with counselors advising new and undecided students and faculty advising students who have declared a major. Whatever the approach, community college leaders know that quality advising and educational planning are critical to student success and to the image of the institution in the community. Advisors are trained to counsel the student concerning development issues, taking his or her major, career goal, off-campus responsibilities, previous educational background, test scores, and motivational level into consideration. Community colleges work with the universities to which their students will transfer to develop transfer manuals, formal articulation agreements, and, in the case of Florida, a *Bill of Rights* for community college transfer students. Some two-year institutions have established articulation offices or transfer centers to help students make the transition to a college or university after earning an AA or AS degree. A few states have legislated mandatory relationships between community colleges and the state university system.

Assessment. Community colleges view testing as one way to measure a student's academic skill level and readiness to learn. The goal of the assessment process is not to exclude applicants but to determine how the institution can best meet a student's needs. Aware that many community college applicants have had bad experiences with tests, student affairs staff members work hard to demystify the testing process, prepare students for the actual test administration, and test in a humane manner. Many community colleges use computer adaptive testing, a process that treats applicants as individuals, customizes the testing process, and stops when a student misses more than a specific number of questions in one area. Most offer an array of workshops to prospective and currently enrolled students to help them deal with test anxiety or to increase their test-taking skills. All work with faculty and staff members to identify and administer entry and exit tests, to develop and monitor the effectiveness of placement models, and to identify students with special educational needs.

Counseling. Because so many community college students enter without clear career direction, view themselves as academically at risk, or face numerous personal challenges that have the potential to interfere with their ability to learn, counseling plays a central role in community college student affairs programs. Undecided students, often 60 percent of each new community college class, increase their probability of staying in college if they identify a major. Counselors offer a variety of services — college credit classes, noncredit career exploration groups, computer-assisted career counseling, self-directed searches, job shadowing, career centers, and cooperative education experiences — to help these students make a career choice. Once they identify a major, students must follow an educational and support service plan that takes into account all of the academic and nonacademic variables that will increase or decrease their prospects for success. Counselors either help students develop such a plan or establish parameters for computer programs that generate individual plans automatically. Students with and without majors need support to succeed in college. Counselors provide this support by offering College Success courses, free workshops on study skills, note-taking, time management, and listening skills, administering tests to help students discover their learning styles, and then instructing them on how to adapt to diverse teaching styles.

Many community college students are in transition in their personal lives but lack the skills to prevent these transitions from interfering with their educational progress. Consequently, personal counseling is an important component of most community college retention programs. This is not therapy but short-term personal counseling to teach coping skills, help students identify alternatives and consequences, and coach students through life challenges that threaten their ability to succeed at the community college.

Financial Aid. Like their counterparts at colleges and universities, most community college students need financial assistance to attend college. Calculating need and creating a financial aid package, however, are only the beginning for community college financial aid offices. Often the first in their families to attend college, many community college students do not know how to complete financial aid forms, develop budgets, establish financial priorities, or manage their money. Some students attend college simply to gain access to loans and grants and do not understand the far-reaching consequences of defaulting on a loan. Others do not comprehend the relationship between financial aid and class performance. To help students use financial aid wisely, community colleges spend a great deal of time creating relationships with students and their families, particularly those who live in low-income areas, long before they apply to the college. Financial aid staff members conduct workshops at schools, churches, and civic organizations for parents and prospective students; coach families through the financial aid application process; assist financial aid recipients to develop and live within realistic budgets; and offer families information about the real costs of college. Hoping to reduce the number of students who graduate from a community college with an enormous loan debt, many community colleges either limit student access to bank loans or counsel against such loans. Because so many of their students are academically at risk, community college financial aid offices often create elaborate student tracking, referral, and early warning systems to identify students in academic trouble in order to create timely intervention and referral opportunities.

Orientation. Most community colleges are commuter institutions whose students view orientation as a necessary evil and want the process to be over as quickly as possible. Their viewpoints are not shared by student affairs staff members who understand that orientation provides an important foundation for student success in two-year institutions. Rather than offer one orientation experience for all students, community colleges offer a variety of options and help applicants select the one that best matches their personal and educational needs. Options include semester-long courses, large and small group sessions offered at strategic times throughout the week, orientation days, pre-packaged Internet and TV sessions, and videos that can be viewed on campus or at home. Many colleges take orientation to the community by offering activities at the job site. Although the delivery systems differ, orientation sessions have the same essential goal: to increase the likelihood that new students will succeed in college.

Community college orientation sessions focus on helping students clarify their educational and career goals, understand their academic strengths and weaknesses in relation to these goals, define educational and support service plans, and develop clear pictures of the institution's expectations and what it will take to succeed in college. Because support systems are extremely important to community college students, many institutions offer orientation sessions for the parents, families, and significant-others of first-term students. These sessions help participants, many of whom have neither attended nor visited a college, to understand the realities of college life, the role they can play in helping family members succeed academically, and the academic and nonacademic assistance available to family members.

Registration and Records. It is in registration and records that community colleges most resemble their college and university counterparts. Records are maintained, residency statements audited, transfer transcripts evaluated, grades recorded, transcripts issued, academic progress tracked, and graduation verified. Most large and mid-size community colleges practice enrollment management, offer telephone registration, receive and send transcripts electronically, and are moving toward paperless systems. Because of the open admissions policy, however, enrollment management in a community college looks different from enrollment management in a university. Community colleges are more likely to target specific programs, areas of the community, or ethnic groups. During years when funding is low, the enrollment management plan may focus on cutting enrollment without endangering programs or the institution's responsibilities to specific subpopulations within the community.

Where community college registration and records staffs differ from their college and university colleagues is in the partnerships they are expected to create with faculty and student affairs colleagues, which are designed to develop, manage, and monitor retention plans that serve to increase the percentage of new students who remain enrolled and who reach their educational goals. At many community colleges, registration and records staff members maintain automated degree audit systems, identify at-risk students and refer them to appropriate interventions, and take the registration process into the community by physically registering students in malls, work sites, or neighborhoods. Innovative registration and records offices at a few community colleges allow students to have access to their records at kiosks throughout the campus or in the community.

Services for Special Populations. Since one of the missions of the community college is to serve those student populations historically under-represented in higher education, almost all of its programs include components designed to meet the needs of students who are members of ethnic minority groups, have a disability, or are entering college to train for a second (or third) career. Almost all community colleges have an office whose primary responsibility is to support students whose disability could interfere with their ability to succeed in college. Most provide targeted services to African American, Asian American, Hispanic, Native American, and international students, either through a special office or as part of existing programs. Child care remains the primary challenge for many community college students, a challenge that cuts across ethnic, gender, and economic boundaries. To truly provide access and opportunity to all, community colleges struggle to help students meet this challenge. Some contract with private providers; others open their own day care centers; a few either use their child development program or create partnerships with community groups; but many, fearful of the impact of child care costs on their budget, offer nothing.

Student Activities. For many community college students, particularly mature adults with family responsibilities, campus life begins when they exit their car and ends when they reach their classroom. Activity programs found at most colleges and universities — rock concerts, Greek life, competitive athletics — hold little attraction for these students. Other students, particularly traditional 18-year old first-year students, complain that community colleges are too much like the high schools from which they recently escaped and do not feel like real colleges. Community college student activities staffs respond by segmenting their market, sponsoring activities that meet the needs of specific target groups, establishing partnerships with the faculty to provide activities and organizations that complement and are incorporated into specific classes, and offering programs on weekends, at lunch, and during breaks between class.

Leadership retreats, often led by college administrators as well as student affairs staff members and the Student Government Association, whose members may be appointed or elected, provide strong foundations for most community college student activity programs. Clubs and organizations, most with significant community service components, are related to various career and academic programs, often meeting in conjunction with a class. Other activities include lunch- or dinner-hour entertainment in the cafeteria, cocurricular lecture series, intramural athletics, weekend plays and concerts, theme weeks that focus on topics of interest to students and their families (substance abuse, parenting, AIDS awareness, safe sex, valuing diversity), seminars and workshops to help students succeed (time management, note taking, test taking), and two or three activities each year to which the entire campus is invited. Many community college student activities programs, particularly those in urban areas, try to connect students with cultural and community activities. The current emphasis on volunteerism in most community colleges is one example of how the student activities staff helps students use their knowledge to help their communities.

LESSONS FROM THE EDGE

As indicated at the beginning of this chapter, college and university leaders can learn a great deal from the experiences of their community college colleagues about identifying and meeting the needs of students from populations historically under-represented in higher education. Student affairs staff members who work in these colleges and universities can learn a great deal about surviving and serving by studying the community college programs described in this monograph. Strong student affairs programs share eleven characteristics. They are:

- proactive and prevention oriented;
- focused on student success;
- targeted to specific student subpopulations;
- based on student needs and action research;
- constantly evolving;
- connected to the teaching-learning process;
- successful at translating theory into practice on a day-by-day basis;
- offered in partnership with on- and off-campus groups;
- practitioner driven;
- guided by the belief that one size does not fit all; and
- committed to simplifying processes, clustering services, and minimizing the number of times a student must come to campus to apply and register.

Moreover, student affairs administrators who thrive in the rapidly changing educational world of the community college create programs and services that:

- Identify the most economical way to deliver services;
- Eliminate outdated student affairs programs, procedures, and traditions;
- Retool practitioners whose skills are outdated;
- Create an equitable procedure within the institution and within the student affairs department to establish priorities and allocate resources;
- Distinguish between services that must be provided by staff members with advanced degrees and services that can be provided by staff members with two- or four-year degrees;
- Define a realistic, defensible role for counselors in the student affairs program;
- Define individual market niches within the comprehensive mission;
- Train faculty members to provide some of the services currently provided by student affairs staff members;
- Use technology to deliver basic services, communicate with internal and external customers, and reduce costs;
- Change rapidly to meet campus and community needs;
- Locate new campus and community partners;
- Develop theories to guide community college student affairs practice with non-white, non-middle-class students;

• Demonstrate their contribution to the institution's bottom line: the ability to attract, retain, and graduate students.

CONCLUSION

If the present for community colleges is the future for colleges and universities — and it is — these institutions must look to their community college neighbors for student affairs programs and practices that meet the needs of students from under-represented populations in all areas: admissions, advising, assessment, counseling, financial aid, orientation, registration and records, services for special populations, and student activities. Rather than replicate these programs, however, colleges and universities must explore their own strengths and weaknesses, identify the best practices in two-year colleges that build on these strengths and minimize the weaknesses, and redirect resources to provide appropriate support services to the latest wave of students from under-represented populations — the challenging students that no one talked about in graduate school.

References

Alfred, R., & Carter, P. (1996). Inside track to the future. *Community College Journal*, 66(4), 10-19.

Baker, G., Roueche, J. E., & Gillett-Karam, R. (1990). *Teaching and leading: Profiles of excellence in the open door college.* Washington, DC: Community College Press.

Chronicle of Higher Education 1997-1998 Almanac. (1997). Washington, DC: *The Chronicle of Higher Education.*

Carnevale, A. P., & Desrochers, D. M. (1997). The role of community colleges in the new economy. *Community College Journal*, 67(5), 27-33.

Conner, L. (1997). The future of community colleges: The good, the bad, the ugly, and the beautiful. In *Celebrations.* Austin, TX: National Institute of Staff and Organizational Development.

Katsinas, S. G. (1994). Is the open door closing? *Community College Journal*, 64(5), 22-28.

Pascarella, E. T. (January-February, 1997). It's time we started paying attention to community college students. *About Campus, 1*, 14-17.

Pascarella, E. T., Edison, M., Nora, A., Hagedorn, L., & Terenzini, P. T. (1995). Cognitive effects of community colleges and four-year colleges. *Community College Journal*, 66(3), 35-39.

Phillippe, K. A. (1995). *National profile of community colleges: Trends and statistics.* Washington, DC: American Association of Community Colleges.

Roueche, J. E., & Roueche, S. D. (1993). *Between a rock and a hard place: The at-risk student in the open-door college.* Washington, DC: American Association of Community Colleges.

Tyree, L. W., & Hellmich, D. M. (1995). Florida's continuing accountability experiment: Yet another community college catch 22. *Community College Journal, 66*(1), 16-20.

CHAPTER TWO

The Student Success Imperative

by Steven R. Helfgot

very few years, we in student affairs go through a process of wringing our hands and searching our souls in the hope of finding some core mission, some central value, some enduring principle around which to organize our work and to which we can dedicate ourselves. We are motivated, it seems, by a deep and recurring need to feel that we are relevant, that we have a place in the academy, that we are a *real* part of our institution's educational mission. Sometimes this need is the reflection of our own insecurity and self-doubt; at other times it comes from questions, often critical questions, that our academic and administrative colleagues regularly ask us.

So, to find our place and to assert our value, we offer up any number of justifications of ourselves and what we do. From the earliest days when our profession was guided by the *Student Personnel Point of View* to today, with the abundance of student development theory that has been the foundation of our work for the last quarter-century, we seem to be on an eternal quest to explain and justify ourselves. That is not all bad, and it is not always merely a defensive reaction: the *Student Personnel Point of View* remains an enduring statement of who we are, what we value, and what we believe about our work with students, and student development theory has taught us much while meaningfully informing our work with students. Yet, the quest continues.

The most notable contemporary manifestation of this continuing quest has been the numerous recent attempts to tie our work more closely to the core academic mission of our institutions: teaching and, to a greater degree, learning. We assert the centrality of the teaching and learning process, offer our support for it, and search desperately for a place for ourselves in that process. The American College Personnel Association's (ACPA) recent *Student Learning Imperative* (American College Personnel Association, 1996) represents one such example. To be critical of *The Student Learning Imperative* is a bit like being critical of God, mom, and apple pie because learning is, of course, at the center of higher education — no one would argue against so obvious a conclusion. That, however, is precisely the starting point for a critical examination of *The Student Learning Imperative*. No one in the academy needs us to tell them that student learning is the most important of institutional goals. It is something that we have all known for some time and that others, most notably faculty and instructional administrators, have been devoted to for as long as there has been higher education in the United States. They have been at it for a long time and, for the most part, do a good job of it.

Supporting student learning is surely the business of every staff member on the college campus, but we in student affairs have another role to play as well, a role for which we are uniquely trained and uniquely suited, one that complements and adds value to a student's education. The function of student affairs staff members is to be facilitators of *student success*. Student success involves more than student learning: it involves the ability to use what has been learned, to apply it, to take it and put it to use in one's life beyond the academic setting.

Student success has been at the center of student affairs practice in the community college for decades. The forms have changed as the definition of success has changed, but helping students to be successful — however that is defined — has been *the* organizing principal for community college student affairs work. Simply stated, this is because community college students are more likely to be at risk than are their counterparts in four-year institutions. Generally speaking, they have fewer advantages and more obstacles to overcome, so they need more help to succeed. As more of those students find their way to university campuses, they will need similar support and help there.

This chapter will look at *The Student Learning Imperative* and compare it to a *Student Success Imperative*, proposing the latter as a more appropriate focus for a student affairs division, especially in institutions with growing populations of nontraditional or new students.

THE STUDENT LEARNING IMPERATIVE

The *Student Learning Imperative* (SLI) is a thoughtful document. Its goals are noble, and its focus on learning is something that no higher education professional would dispute. The problem, especially for student affairs administrators in community colleges, is that it rests on assumptions about students that are not always true. It has limited utility because it seems to write off many typical community college students although, ironically, from the viewpoint of a community college student affairs practitioner, it begins with great promise, asserting that "increased numbers of people from historically under-represented groups [are] going to college" (ACPA, 1996, p. 118). These are the students who populate community colleges and who are, increasingly, appearing on university campuses, some as transfer students and others as first-year students. So, while the SLI acknowledges the presence of new or nontraditional students, it seems to make the erroneous assumption that they are like or will become like more traditional students.

At one point, the SLI states that when student affairs staff members discourage students from spending time and energy on nonproductive pursuits, and encourage them to use institutional resources (e. g., libraries, student organizations, laboratories, studios), to employ effective learning strategies (e. g., study time, peer tutors), and to participate in community governance and other educationally purposeful activities, the students learn more (ACPA, 1996, p. 119). The implication is clear. Student affairs staff members should be encouraging students to spend more time on campus, in activities — both curricular and extracurricular — that lead to students learning more, and more effectively. This is entirely reasonable if, and only if, one assumes that the students being so encouraged are traditional students. Clearly, students who are full time, who reside on campus, who do not need to work (or work only part time, on campus), who have as their only real responsibility the pursuit of a degree, could respond to this encouragement. They might, for example, be helped to see the value of spending the afternoon in the library instead of in front of the TV watching soap operas or a ball game, or that free time would be better used participating in a student organization than in shooting pool in the student center.

With nontraditional students, however, such encouragement might be both ineffective and, more important, inappropriate, perhaps even discouraging them rather than encouraging them. Our efforts to move students toward more educationally purposeful activities might be perceived as instituting yet another set of obstacles they cannot overcome, another set of goals they cannot achieve. Imagine, for example, a fairly typical community college student, 27 years old and a single mother of two. Each semester she attempts to find one course, or maybe two, that will not be in conflict with her work schedule and the availability of child care. She arrives on campus just in time for class to begin and leaves the moment class is over. How much time she has to study on any given day — if any — depends on how much time and attention her children need in the evening, on how early they get to sleep, and on how much work she must get done around the house. To what educationally purposeful activities should we direct her? And what help do we offer her by operating from a model that suggests that the ways in which she spends her time are not productive and not likely to enhance her learning?

For students such as this, still nontraditional on university campuses but in the mainstream at community colleges, learning is unquestionably important. More important than learning itself, however, is becoming successful, in whatever way they define success: getting a job in the field for which they have been training while in school; getting into the university (with the necessary financial aid); or earning sufficient credit hours in the right courses to get a promotion at work. In that light, consider the following characteristics of "The Learning Oriented Student Affairs Division" (ACPA, 1996).

- The student affairs division's mission complements the institution's mission, with the enhancement of student learning and personal development being the primary goal of student affairs programs and services.
- Resources are allocated to encourage student learning and personal development.
- Student affairs professionals collaborate with other institutional agents and agencies to promote student learning and personal development.
- The division of student affairs includes staff members who are experts on students, their environments, and teaching and learning processes.
- Student affairs policies and programs are based on promising practices from research on student learning and institution-specific assessment data.

It is important to keep in mind that there is absolutely nothing wrong with any of the above characteristics or with the idea of a learning-oriented student affairs division, in the proper context. The problem is the inaccurate assumption that such a context — one in which traditional students are the norm — is the only context or even the typical context for American higher education. In fact, both two- and four-year campuses that are populated by nontraditional students are, increasingly, the norm: The student success imperative, which will be introduced below, is more appropriate in *this* context.

THE STUDENT SUCCESS IMPERATIVE

It could be argued that if students are learning, then they are being successful. The object of colleges and universities is, after all, to impart knowledge to students and for students to assimilate that knowledge, i.e., to learn. In truth though, especially for highly pragmatic, goal oriented, meat and potatoes community college students, learning is only a part, albeit a central part, of what it means to be successful. Success for many of them is not in learning itself but in the ability to do something with what has been learned. Given their overall orientation, success is using what has been learned to achieve some larger and more specific goal, and this is the yardstick by which many community college students measure the student services which are provided.

Definitions of success can be grand or mundane and may change over time. In the 1960s, success was defined for many community college students in terms put forth by the human potential movement: self-awareness, self-actualization, the realization of one's potential in psychological and humanistic terms. In the 1970s and into the 1980s, as the economy fluctuated, with inflation rising and falling along with unemployment, success for many community college students was defined in terms of economics. Did one acquire both the academic and personal skills needed to obtain and hold a well paying and secure job?

Today, as community college student bodies continue to become increasingly diverse, the definitions of success are equally diverse. For the new immigrant — whether aged 18 or 68 — success may be defined as having the basic literacy skills that allow a person to function, at some minimal level at least, in society. For the middle-aged male who has worked for the whole of his adult life in the steel mills of the Midwest or in an aerospace or defense plant in California, success may mean doing whatever is required to develop skills that will lead to a new job, and to do so as quickly as possible. For them, it may not even matter what the work is, as long as it will pay the mortgage, put food on the table, and pay the kids' college tuition. For the economically disadvantaged but academically able high school graduate coming to the community college, success may be defined as the opportunity to complete general education requirements for transfer to the university while working full time, and to earn enough money to be able to afford to attend the university once the transfer requirements are completed. For the welfare recipient, success is *beating the clock*, developing sufficient skill to get work — work that pays more than welfare — before the date at which welfare payments stop. For the woman in middle age, perhaps newly widowed or divorced or confronting an empty nest, success may be the opportunity to find purpose and meaning through learning for its own sake, or to prepare to return to a career, long ago abandoned, or anticipated for half a lifetime. And for the 22 year-old high school dropout, perhaps caught in a dead-end job, success may be defined as being able to get through one college course, any college course.

In each of these cases, learning is a central component but learning, mastery of subject matter, is not in and of itself success. Said differently, learning is a necessary condition for success, but it is not by itself sufficient to define success. It is hard to imagine that these students, defining success as they do, would be interested in, understand, or have the time for educationally purposeful activities.

If these remarkably diverse community college students have varying definitions of success in the larger context of life, career, and purpose, they have perhaps even greater diversity in their more everyday and mundane definitions of success. Though there are surely some community college students for whom learning and the enhancement of learning are the heart of the matter, there are many others for whom success on a daily, weekly, or a semester's basis is expressed in very simple terms, and sometimes in terms of very real fears:

- I hope that I pass all my classes this semester.
- I don't want to have to drop any of my classes this semester.
- How do I get financial aid?
- Will these classes lead me to a job?
- How can I transfer to the university when I have to work 40 hours a week and they don't have night classes?
- How can I convince my parents that it's worthwhile for me to stay in school rather than go to work?
- How do I dress for and what do I say in a job interview?
- I don't have the money for books; how do I keep up with my work until I get the money?
- I know that the final is tomorrow, but my baby is sick and I don't have anyone to help me.

None of this is very grand nor intellectually rich. None of it speaks to great academic or intellectual achievements. Success here is not defined in terms of mastering research techniques, or understanding profound ideas, but in everyday, real life terms by people who are living real lives every day. These are people for whom student is only one role of many and not, of necessity, the most important role.

To be of genuine service, student services administrators need to embrace the goal of student success and to do so in students' own terms. As much as we might like to facilitate intellectual growth, as much as we might like to help students immerse themselves in and fall in love with learning (perhaps as we were helped, leading to our own careers as educators), as much as we might want to help every student become part of a learning community, we have to step back and determine when those are genuinely the student's goals and desires and when they are *our* goals for the student. When it is the latter, we need to refocus ourselves on the student's notions of success, even if they are as basic as those described above. We must see these students as something other than marginal; we must see them as real students and believe, along with them, that they can achieve their goals. Our work with them may not be to facilitate increased involvement in educationally purposeful activities. It may just mean helping them get by. Such work becomes of great professional value, however, when we are guided by a student success imperative with the following characteristics.

The student affairs division's mission complements the institution's mission by encouraging, developing, and facilitating activities to promote and ensure student success as the primary goal of student affairs programs and services.

Many colleges define their overall mission in terms of learning, intellectual development, and, sometimes, personal development. In a community college student affairs division focused on student success, the single most important role for student affairs staff members becomes that of helping students translate and apply what they have learned. In this way, the student affairs division complements the institution's mission.

The translation may involve, for example, helping students to understand how their own knowledge can lead to a job, and, even more important, to learn and apply the skills necessary to get a job. Community college students may complete one of many career programs, in such varied fields as automotive technology, culinary arts, court reporting, nursing, welding, and paralegal studies. A student with a straight "A" average, however, may have absolutely no idea of what is required to get a job in a particular field. Student affairs staff members can show that vocational student how to apply what has been learned to achieve success, helping the student construct a resume that is appropriate for both the field and a specific job. They will help the student prepare for an interview, learn how to "dress for success," develop self-confidence and interpersonal skills, and understand proper workplace behavior.

All of this may appear rather mundane and commonplace. Every college and university — both two- and four-year — has a career center and career placement services. Typically, though, these career services are available only if the student seeks them out. Many nontraditional students have no knowledge of, or experience with, seeking out professional positions; career planning activities are not part of their world. They cannot rely on parents and other relatives to guide them toward these services, for, in many cases, their relatives also are without experience in these areas. So, career services in a student success oriented student affairs division must be proactive rather than reactive, seeking out students and finding ways to ensure that services are delivered. For instance, some community colleges have added a career planning course, provided by career services, as a program requirement for those with vocational majors. Others have included a career planning module as part of another course in the major, recognizing that simply learning welding or court reporting or nursing is not enough. Students need to know how to get a job where they can use those skills. The student affairs division, in this case through career services, adds value, complements the instructional mission, and helps the student move beyond learning to success.

The same is true for students planning to transfer to a university. Many community college students, including those who are the first in their family to go to college and those who come from disadvantaged backgrounds, achieve at a very high academic level. If they are going to be in school, using what often are limited family resources, then they are going to make the most of it. They work hard; they get the very best grades; they excel. They can do so because they have experience in going to school. Making the transition from high school to the community college can be a real challenge, though, because there are some differences, and transferring from the community college to the university can pose an even greater challenge.

As students move from elementary school to junior high school to high school, the transitions are easy; they are told where and when to show up, and the school assumes most of the responsibility. To enter the community college, however, the students have to initiate activity: file an application, perhaps arrange for assessment tests and an orientation or counseling appointment, select classes and register for them. For many — even those with the best of grade point averages — these are unfamiliar activities. Understanding this, the outreach and admissions offices in many community colleges bring the application and admission process to local high schools, so that students are not overwhelmed or scared away or simply do not apply because they are embarrassed by not knowing what to do.

If the process of applying to the open door community college can be daunting for nontraditional students, then applying to the university as a transfer student can be nearly overwhelming. Imagine the student who has completed all of the course work for transfer from the community college and has earned a grade point average of 3.65 in the process. By that standard, the student has clearly learned. Although this student wants to transfer to the university, he or she knows little about how and when to apply to the university, and even less about how to apply for financial aid, how to obtain housing, etc. For this student, success is not synonymous with an outstanding grade point average or even with all that has been learned: success is being able to use that GPA to get into (and eventually complete) a degree at the university. And it will be members of the student affairs staff — advisors, and others — at the community college who will help this student navigate the process of transferring to the university. They start with a student who has learned, to be sure, and help the student to move on to the next step and to exploit what has been learned.

One concrete example of how this works is the Transfer Mentor program at Cerritos College in California. In this program, students from Cerritos who have successfully transferred to public or private universities agree to serve as mentors to students in the transfer process. These mentors return to Cerritos to participate in panel discussions, offering a student's eye view of life at the university, and giving those about to transfer inside information and survival tips. Additionally, each mentor agrees to work one-on-one with a new transfer student to help him or her through the first semester or year at the university. The program is coordinated by a member of the School and Community Relations Division. Student services staff members at the universities help identify and even train potential mentors.

With community college students, and those like them who are becoming more numerous on four-year campuses, old assumptions no longer hold. Students will learn; the instructional mission will be fulfilled. Student affairs staff members, however, must play a complementary and proactive role by helping students take advantage of the knowledge they have gained through successful movement into employment or further education or, in many cases, both.

Resources are allocated to those things that provide added opportunities for students to reach both their immediate and long-term goals successfully.

Student services administrators are uncomfortable with the thought that resources *within* the student services division may have to be redirected or redistributed. Only slightly worse is the concern that we might have to change, perhaps even significantly change, what we do to maintain or enlarge our role in the institution. Both of these ideas, however, are central to the creation of and support for a student success oriented student affairs division.

In such a division, the staff has clear, accurate, and regularly updated information and data about students, their goals, and what success means to them in both the short and long term. Programs and services need not be eliminated but they may have to change, be redesigned to be responsive and flexible, positioned to accommodate shifting student needs. For example, as resources are allocated to and within the student activities program, fewer dollars may go to concerts and film series or fraternities and sororities, and more may go to clubs and organizations that support the curriculum and increase students' chances to be successful in getting a job. Less money may go to a spring carnival and more to a spring career fair. Fewer dollars may go toward weekend ski trips and more toward expanding the hours of the library and child care center.

Counseling centers and their work must be focused on student goals and those things that students require to be successful. Academic counseling and planning may play a large role for students who need help in planning their courses and schedules efficiently and accurately. Providing academic counseling, however, may not always be the professional priority of counselors who may be more interested in developmental or even therapeutic counseling. Indeed, this is one of the distinctions between those who work in counseling centers on two-year campuses and in four-year counseling centers. Community college counselors are much more likely to be academic counselors while those at universities are much more likely to deal with developmental or mental health issues. As the student population at senior institutions begins to look more and more like the population at community colleges, however, it is possible that those students will be asking more for academic than for personal assistance. If that is, in fact, the case, where will the resources go? On many campuses, an advising center exists separately from the counseling center. Will it get a larger portion of the budget and the counseling center a smaller share, or will the counseling center redesign itself to offer more academic counseling and support?

In fairness, a counseling center that has a student success focus, whether at a community college or a university, will not simply provide academic counseling. Since community college students often balance (although sometimes just barely) work, family, and school commitments, workshops and seminars on time management and stress management may be invaluable to helping them succeed in their goals.

Similarly, students whose families have no history of college attendance, as well as those from certain ethnic and cultural backgrounds, may find that the role of college student comes into conflict with other roles they are expected to fulfill. Their values, traditions, and standards of behavior may change. They may be less available, or unavailable, to their family when they have to prepare for an exam, write a paper, or participate in a study group. Such situations may cause the student to turn to the college counseling center for assistance in resolving the tensions. Similar situations may be faced by counseling centers working with traditional students, but with community college students these conflicts are often not matters of personal development alone but conflicts that call into question the student's ability to remain in school. A counselor may need to work with family or community members to help the student succeed. Resources will have to be allocated to whatever counseling services — academic, career, or personal — can help students meet their goals. Such goals may be short term and immediate, such as being able to remain in school, or long term, such as developing the patience to pursue a degree one course at a time; what is important is that service goals, efforts, and allocations of personnel, time, and money be directed by the students' needs and definitions of success.

Student affairs administrators work in partnership with those inside the institution (including students, faculty, administrators, and service providers) and those outside (including families, employers, local government, social service agencies, civic groups, high schools, and other colleges and universities) to help remove obstacles to and provide greater opportunities for student success.

Elsewhere in this monograph, authors discuss partnerships and their importance to student affairs programs focused on student success, especially in community colleges. Such partnerships are so centrally important that they will also be discussed here.

There are many clichés about higher education, and, like all clichés, they have a grain of truth to them. Students, for example, are often said to be on their own at college, adults now, who are responsible for themselves. No one will check up on them, monitor them, tell them what to do or when to do it. They will make their own decisions and they will live with the consequences. There is truth in this notion to be sure, and for those of us in student affairs, who gave up *in loco parentis* decades ago, it rings especially true. Yet, for students new to college, first-time college-goers with multiple responsibilities outside of school who risk failure for any number of possible reasons, the assumption that they are on their own, to sink or swim, may be inappropriate. If student success is the goal of the student affairs division, then students who need assistance — even aggressive, intrusive assistance — should get it. For many, their needs may go beyond the capacities of the student affairs division, requiring the development of partnerships both within and outside the institution.

For many faculty members who were trained to teach traditional college students and who have spent years teaching those students, coping with new types of students can be problematic. They are used to imposing absolute deadlines for papers and projects, under the assumption that nothing could possibly be more important to a student than the exam they have scheduled for a particular day and time, and accustomed to students who behave in a certain way in class. These assumptions and expectations no longer hold for many students in community colleges and for increasing numbers of students in senior institutions. The demand to meet a deadline for a paper will not be compelling for a student who faces a similar deadline for a major project at work. The demands of a final exam cannot compete with those of a sick child or of a last-minute business trip. Students from other cultures will not necessarily respond in class in the ways that faculty expect; they may not be comfortable speaking out, offering their opinions, or challenging authority.

Student affairs administrators who know and understand these students and who are committed to their success will not only act as advocates on their behalf, but will develop partnerships with the faculty to help them succeed. They will help faculty members understand the developmental, learning, and life issues that nontraditional students bring to college. They will consult with faculty colleagues to help them make accommodations for the real needs of these students while maintaining the integrity of their classes. Student affairs staff and faculty members must work in partnership to assure that their students have the opportunity to succeed.

Along with partnerships with faculty, student affairs administrators need to work together with administrators and other service providers in the institution. There is no need to dwell on this at length. Those in student affairs who advocate for student success must work with administrators who develop class schedules, write institutional policies, hire staff members, and establish the hours during which offices are open. Working students have no chance to be successful if, for example, the classes they need are not available when they can attend class. Similarly, nontraditional students cannot be successful if the policies that have the greatest impact on them are written with the assumption that all students are traditional. Students who need tutoring, learning assistance, career counseling, or financial aid to succeed have little or no chance to do so if those services are only available at hours convenient for traditional full-time students.

Community colleges are commuter institutions, which makes them appealing to nontraditional students who live in those communities. The majority of these students will continue to reside with their families and work in their communities, commuting to school. To help these students have the greatest chance for success, student affairs administrators must, on occasion, look beyond the students themselves to individuals and groups in the community who interact with and influence them; then must view these influential members of the student's world as partners in helping the students achieve success.

High schools should be seen as more than just sources of students. Understanding high schools can help colleges understand students and the communities from which they come: discussions of curriculum, student readiness, and the level or lack of support from families can help student affairs administrators better understand their students, meet their needs, and help them succeed. Reaching out to and involving parents can be similarly useful. Parents who are unfamiliar with the realities of college life — for example, that on some days a student may not have classes, or that before final exams a student may be uncommunicative and unavailable — may sometimes, inadvertently, make things more difficult for students. College staff members who recruit parents as allies and help them understand the meaning of attending college can help ease tensions at home, removing obstacles and increasing the possibilities of student success.

For older students who are themselves spouses, parents, and employees, similar issues can emerge. In such cases though, student affairs administrators may turn to the husbands or wives and children of students as well as their employers. Helping them to be understanding and supportive of students in whatever ways possible and enlisting them as partners can improve the chances for student success.

Some community college students are also social service clients. Workers who have lost their jobs and are collecting unemployment often turn to the community college to learn new job skills and prepare for a new career. Welfare recipients turn to community college training programs to prepare themselves for jobs and independence. Today, welfare recipients in new welfare-to-work programs represent a significant new wave of community college students. Whatever their particular situation, these students have obstacles to overcome. A student affairs division focused on student success can take the lead in coordinating assistance with social service agencies and government agencies. Together they can work to help students get the education they want and need, coordinating schedules and benefits, such as child care, and removing whatever barriers exist. In this way, all win.

Cooperative relationships between colleges and universities can make a real contribution to student success — most obviously in arrangements that ease the transfer process, such as articulation agreements, campus visits by university recruiters, transfer guarantees, and on-site field admissions. Other opportunities exist as well. As more and more nontraditional students move into the university, discussions, workshops, and seminars should bring staff members from institutions that have long served such students together with those from institutions that have only recently begun to enroll them. Further, cooperative arrangements that allow students with busy schedules and multiple demands on their time to take courses at several nearby institutions during the same semester can be of tremendous benefit to students. One semester it may be most convenient for a student to enroll in a course close to home; the next semester it may be much more convenient to enroll in a course nearer to the workplace. If formal agreements exist to allow students to do this, so much the better but even where there are no such agreements, counselors, academic advisors or even admissions office staff members can work together to make such opportunities more readily available to students.

Partnerships are vital to student success, both inside the college and out. Perhaps most important is an attitude of openness to pursuing partnerships that will benefit students wherever those opportunities present themselves.

The division of student affairs includes staff members who are experts on students, their communities and cultures, on teaching and learning, on advocacy, and on the resources available, in both college and community, to help students to be successful. In large part, this point is a logical extension of the preceding one. While its meaning may seem obvious, several points must be made explicit.

Student affairs divisions that are genuinely concerned about student success will hire staff members whose expertise encompasses the widely diverse student populations who may enroll in their institutions. Alternatively, and perhaps more important, they will provide opportunities for staff members to develop expertise concerning students and their cultures and communities, especially at times when the student population is in a state of flux. Students from diverse backgrounds are taking advantage of higher education, often more quickly than theories about and descriptions of them can be developed and presented in the literature. Student affairs staff members learn about students from first-hand campus experience. Opportunities to develop such expertise have to be made available, a priority that should be made a part of departmental job descriptions. Although this is difficult, insofar as it requires substantially more effort than merely staying current with the literature, it is central to student success.

Although student affairs staff members should look beyond student learning to the wider concept of student success, they should not be ignorant about teaching and learning but must be experts on learning theory, learning styles, and teaching methods. Learning is the heart of the academic enterprise, and students have little or no chance to succeed in the broader sense if they cannot succeed in learning. Student affairs staff members need to be conversant with the essential elements of teaching and learning.

Success is ultimately the responsibility of students themselves, but they may need help to reach that goal. In some situations, help may take the form of advocacy. Effective advocacy — whether inside the institution or outside — depends on several things. First, those who hope to act as advocates for students must know and understand them. Second, they must know and understand those to whom they are going to advocate on students' behalf. Internally, that means they must know the college and its structure, administrators and administrative policies, faculty and faculty needs, and the essential elements of teaching and learning. Externally, student advocates need to know and understand families and cultures, communities and employers, their various expectations for demands upon students, and their relationship with the college and its mission. The advocate will, of course, be more effective if he or she is seen as a friend and partner rather than an adversary or opponent. This highlights, yet again, the importance of partnerships for those who see student success as their core mission.

To understand what form advocacy might take inside the college or university, recall some of the earlier points about students who have other commitments that might supersede those to a course on a given day. Student affairs staff members who are focused on student success may at times need to play an advocate's role for students with faculty or administrators to help them understand that standards of appropriate student behavior and student expectations change as student populations change. Thus, student affairs administrators will not suggest that students be excused from assignments and exams or be held to different standards, but they may seek to obtain more flexible schedules and deadlines as well as greater options for students.

Advocacy for students that goes beyond the campus often involves some of the same issues that require advocacy on campus. Student affairs administrators may persuade an employer to be more flexible in assigning a work schedule and to avoid shifting a student's hours in the middle of a semester, or even to allow the college to schedule classes at the work site. Campus advocates may interact with caseworkers and other social service providers to encourage services, policies, and procedures that will support student-clients. Advocates for students may also seek out local churches and other religious institutions, which have great influence in many communities and cultures. If religious leaders understand, endorse, and explain the requirements and benefits of college, some of the pressures placed on student members of their congregation can be relieved, allowing their potential for success to grow.

Direct advocacy with families may be necessary, although there may be problems even after family members are enlisted as partners in support of a student. Conflicts may arise over the long hours the student spends studying on campus, weekends spent working on group projects, or they may result from differences in values. One woman student with whom I worked was preparing to transfer, having decided she wanted the full college experience during her final two years in school. She had worked for several years and had saved sufficient money to enable her to live on the university campus, and that decision created an immense conflict within her family, with her father in particular. In the culture of the country from which her family had come, unmarried women did not leave home. If she left, he said, she would be disowned by the family. The conflict was finally resolved positively, partly because a staff member with the same cultural background intervened with the father on the student's behalf.

There are numerous components to student success. Knowing, understanding, and supporting students is important and advocacy may be essential. Being able to connect students to sources and resources — on campus and off — is equally important. Helping students succeed may necessitate actions as simple and traditional as referring them to the counseling center, the tutoring center, or to a stress management workshop, but may also involve referrals to community services that may be less familiar to the traditionally-oriented student affairs staff member.

A student may not be able to stay in school without access to short-term emergency child care, for example, if that student's regular child care is not available; a student without medical insurance may become ill and be in danger of missing days or weeks of school unless medical care can be obtained. A student affairs professional who knows the student and the community may be able to refer the student to a free clinic or to low-cost medical care. Consider, too, the student who is both a spouse and a parent and has a family that is in serious crisis. Such problems can become overwhelming, even debilitating, so the student could well lose his or her focus on and interest in school. Many college counseling centers do not offer marital or family counseling, but those services are available in most communities. Student affairs administrators familiar with community resources might be able to refer a student and his or her family to an agency or private practitioner for counseling support that might be enough to enable the student to stay focused on and remain in school while the crisis is being resolved.

Essentially, student affairs administrators will continue to rely on their traditional expertise, but they will need to expand their repertoire of knowledge, skills, resources, and contacts to help nontraditional students succeed.

Student affairs policies and programs are based primarily on accurate information about the institution's students and community, on practices shown to contribute to student success, and on an assessment of what is needed by current students to successfully reach their goals, consistent with the college's educational mission.

For years colleges and universities assumed that what was true about their students in the past was still true in the present and would continue to be true in the future. For some institutions — those which can be very selective and truly manage their enrollment — this may remain an accurate assumption, but for many of today's colleges and universities, and for community colleges for virtually their entire history, the assumption is wholly inaccurate. For these schools, the student population is ever-changing. As changes occur, student affairs administrators must constantly renew their knowledge base about students and their needs, about their communities, and about the programs and services that will help them. What met the needs of adult women may not be effective, for example, with people changing careers or with new immigrants. Conversely, some programs and services that helped one group may work well with another. Programs, services, departments, and the whole student affairs division may need to change the substance of their activities, the job descriptions of staff members, and the structure of their organization as students and their needs change.

A student affairs division that is oriented toward student success takes the lead in determining what is true and what is not, what works and what does not. Interviews, assessments, focus groups, formal research studies, and program evaluations and assessments can all assist the student affairs division and the college as a whole in helping students to be successful, and, in turn, allow the institution to do some soul-searching about itself and its mission. Does that mission meet the needs of the students currently attending? If not, should the mission change or should the college make a concerted effort to reconfigure its student body? These are not simple questions, but without the information that comes from really knowing students and being genuinely concerned for their success, the opportunity to ask and answer them will not become available. Without such inquiries, there is a danger that the institution can lose touch with its students and become stagnant.

The student affairs division, whenever possible and appropriate to the student's situation, encourages and provides opportunities for students to engage in activities that enhance learning and promote personal development.

This last point brings the notion of a student success imperative full circle to meet the central ideal of *The Student Learning Imperative*. Indeed, the success imperative does not in the least suggest that the goals of the SLI are unimportant or lack value — quite the contrary. If the situation allows, with either a traditional student or nontraditional student, student affairs staff members should always help students find and engage in activities that enhance learning and development. In working with nontraditional students, there would be no greater triumph than to see them arrive at a stage where they can pursue activities oriented toward these goals.

Consider, again, the example of the student who, having finished her work at the community college, wanted to transfer to the university, live on campus, and have a complete college experience. Even though she ran into an obstacle, once that obstacle was overcome, she did move on campus and she did have that experience. Most important is the ability to distinguish between students who have reached a stage in their lives where they can immerse themselves in their education, and those whose situations, like most described in this chapter, do not allow such a focus. To help the former students focus on educationally purposeful activities and activities that enhance personal development is a service; to do so with the latter group of students is to do them a disservice.

Student affairs staff members need to be cautious in two respects. First, they must accurately assess which type of situation a student is in and avoid pushing students toward activities that would be inappropriate for them. Second, student affairs staff members have to be equally careful not to imply that students who are in a position to immerse themselves in their education and related activities more fully are somehow superior to or more serious than those who are not. Student success must remain the focal point, and students define success differently according to their circumstances, their background, and their current life situation. Our profession has always recognized and valued the importance of individual differences. Today there is, perhaps, a wider range of differences in students than ever before, requiring a wider range of responses. One size does not fit all, and a focus on enhanced learning is not appropriate for all.

CONCLUSION

College is no longer the exclusive domain of 18-22 years olds who live on campus and go to school full time. This has been the reality at community colleges for years and is increasingly becoming the reality at many four-year colleges and universities. Student populations are increasingly diverse, and the way they view education and the place of education in their lives is similarly diverse. In our seemingly endless efforts to define the place of student affairs in the academy, we look for a purpose, a theme, a value to which we can attach ourselves. Committing ourselves to the centrality of learning is one such purpose, one perhaps best exemplified by *The Student Learning Imperative*.

Important as *The Student Learning Imperative* is, however, it is also limiting. The SLI may not be appropriate for all students and may, in fact, be discouraging to them, making them feel inadequate. A student success imperative that accounts for a more diverse student population with various needs and with various definitions of success provides a better focus for student affairs administrators. Such a focus allows the student affairs division to offer added value to student learning and permits student affairs staff members to help students maximize their learning and put it to practical use — to be successful. To paraphrase the cliché: *No one can argue with success!*

References
American College Personnel Association. The student learning imperative: Implications for student affairs. (1996). *Journal of College Student Development, 37*, 118-122.

CHAPTER THREE

— ◆ —

Translating Theory into Practice

by Linda Reisser

As Chapter One demonstrates, community colleges differ from colleges and universities in mission, organizational structure, curriculum, and students. They are often the first to register demographic, social, political, and economic changes. Because of their accessibility, diversity, and community connections, they can provide early warning signs of the waves that are rolling toward four-year institutions. Because of their flexibility and adaptability, community colleges know from experience what works and what does not in trying to respond to growing demands with limited resources. Four-year institutions are already feeling the approach of the wave, and will continue to face the challenges that community colleges have been coping with for some time, including:

- more pressure on professional staff members to improve programs and maintain services with fewer resources;
- an aging faculty and staff — some approaching retirement and others invested in past practices;
- more adult students seeking programs and services relevant to their needs; more diverse students, including those who need additional support services, tutoring, or developmental math and English; more women and minorities; and
- the changing social, economic, and psychological barriers to student success.

THE IMPORTANCE OF THEORY

Theory should play a vital role in student affairs. First, the use of theory provides a useful lens for observing, describing, and investigating student characteristics, and for identifying underlying patterns of thinking, feeling, knowing, and behaving. Second, it can suggest strategies for promoting student learning and for understanding and managing change in individuals, small groups, and organizations. Third, theory should provide a foundation for predicting and assessing the impact of programs and for generating new research and further theory. Perhaps a more intangible reason that theory is important is that it should remind professionals of their most important goal: beyond processing forms and meeting enrollment goals, student affairs practitioners aim to transform lives. Challenging students and supporting the growth of knowledge and competence is a lofty ideal. Theory can help by focusing on how this happens and thus how conscious decisions can be made to help it happen more effectively.

With all that theory can offer, it nonetheless seems to be rarely applied in daily practice. A familiar refrain is that practitioners are too busy solving problems and providing services to keep up to date with theory, let alone to design and evaluate programs that are theory-driven. They may have done so as an exercise in graduate school, but many did not go through graduate programs in student personnel administration. Those who got an overview of theory may have seen it as providing an interesting approach to cognitive or psychosocial development but do not see how to apply it outside of a classroom setting, especially given that theories of intellectual and ethical development seem more applicable to work with cohort groups, where changes in thinking and valuing can be observed over a period of time. Other theories or research updates may remain on the shelf because of the scholarly context within which they were generated. As Upcraft (1993) writes:

> The gap between theory and practice does not arise entirely from the fact that busy practitioners have no time for reading. Researchers, academicians, and theoreticians are frequently guilty of writing in ways that though contributing to the scholarly literature, do little to help the practitioner. It appears to some that real scholarship disdains the practical and that it is in part defined by how specialized, esoteric, complex, and irrelevant to practice it is. Scholars developing theory are often so isolated from campus realities that their ideas have little to do with campus problems and issues (p. 265).

Theory may not be seen as applicable unless it generates principles or conceptual tools that can easily be held in mind and used consciously to inform practice. For example, the concepts of *challenge and support* and *student involvement in learning* gave practitioners compasses for mapping a broad variety of programs. Other theories have been applicable in specific areas; Holland's theory of vocational personalities and work environments, for example, may be of great interest to those working in the area of career exploration, but is unknown to those with more generalist interests. Similarly, interest in applying the Myers-Briggs typological theory has been growing and has encouraged more practitioners to attend workshops or receive in-depth training and certification to administer the inventory, yet few practitioners would view this theory as useful for program-design, especially given the no-frills programs which often best meet the needs of community college students.

Theory may also be viewed as irrelevant to today's diverse students. Many current practitioners remember studying earlier theoretical models by Sanford, Erikson, Chickering, Perry, Loevinger, and Kolb, which either reflected a more clinical, psychological approach to development or were based on a narrow sample of males or females at small, liberal arts colleges. In the 1980s, theories emerged to address the development of groups excluded from earlier models — women, ethnic groups, older students, gay and lesbian students, commuters, and others, but practitioners may not have had the opportunity to review them or may be intimidated by the challenge of distinguishing one from another.

Another barrier to applying theory, particularly in community colleges, is that practitioners are not rewarded for generating theory and research, let alone for updating their own knowledge base. Theoretical studies and research are conducted primarily in four-year institutions with graduate programs, and such work is often designed with neither nontraditional students nor the people who work with them in mind. Yet, there are many opportunities for practitioners at both two-year and four-year institutions to attend conferences, read journals, and hold discussions about how to adapt existing theories to foster student development more effectively, and such theories have much to offer.

Over the past 25 years, research has unequivocally documented how college has an impact on both cognitive and affective development. Key aspects of institutional behavior and characteristics associated with powerful educational environments have been identified. Pascarella and Terenzini (1991) summarize those findings:

> A reasonably consistent set of cognitive, attitudinal, value and psychosocial
> changes have occurred among college students over the last four or five decades.
> Students learn to think in more abstract, critical, complex, and reflective ways;
> there is a general liberalization of values and attitudes combined with an increase
> in cultural and artistic interests and activities; progress is made toward the
> development of personal identities and more positive self-concepts; and there is an
> expansion and extension of interpersonal horizons, intellectual interests, individual

autonomy, and general psychological maturity and well-being . . .

Perhaps the clearest generalization to be made . . . is that on nearly all of the
dimensions on which we find freshman-to-senior change, a statistically significant
part of that change is attributable to college attendance, not to rival explanations. .
. . These effects cannot be explained away by maturation or differences between
those who attend and those who do not attend college in intelligence, academic
ability, or other precollege characteristics (pp. 563- 564).

If human development is the unifying purpose for higher education, then
practitioners should focus resources on activities most likely to foster student learning. The many relevant theoretical frames of reference can be clus-
tered into four broad categories.
   • Psychosocial theories view development as a series of developmental
   tasks or stages, involving qualitative changes in thinking, feeling, behaving, valuing, and relating to others and to oneself. Theories by Erikson,
   Chickering, Marcia, Heath, Cross, and Josselson belong in this group.
   • Cognitive theories describe changes in thinking and the evolving frames
   of reference which structure values, beliefs, and assumptions, such as
   movement away from passive, receptive, concrete, superficial thinking
   toward more active, creative, abstract, in-depth, objective, and complex
   ways of engaging with subject matter or making ethical judgments. Examples include theories proposed by Perry, Belenky, Clinchy, Goldberger
   and Tarule, Baxter Magolda, Kohlberg, Gilligan, Loevinger, Kegan, Fowler,
   and Kitchener, and King.
   • Typological theories describe the distinctive but stable differences in
   learning style, personality type, temperament, or socioeconomic background that provide contexts for development. Among these theories are
   those formulated by Kolb, Myers-Briggs, Keirsey, and K.P. Cross.
   • Person-environment interaction theories focus on how the environment
   influences behavior through its interactions with characteristics of the individual. Examples include campus ecology theories, Holland's Theory
   of Vocational Personalities and Work Environments, and other perceptual
   models.

AN APPLICABLE THEORY
Chickering's Seven Vectors

Chickering's model, in which he proposed seven vectors of development in
college students, continues to offer a holistic theory which can easily be applied in both two-year and four-year institutions. His book, *Education*

Figure 5.1
The Seven Vectors
General Developmental Directions

From	To
Developing Competence • Low level of competence (intellectual, physical, interpersonal) • Lack of confidence in one's abilities	• High level of competence in each area • Strong sense of competence
Managing Emotions • Little control over disruptive emotions and impulses • Inability to access the full range of feelings	• Flexible control and appropriate expression • Ability to feel and accept the full range of feelings
Moving through Autonomy toward Independence • Emotional dependence • Poor self-direction or inability to or confidence to be mobile • Independence	• Freedom from continual and pressing needs for reassurance • Instrumental autonomy (inner direction, persistence, and mobility) • Recognition and acceptance of the importance of interdependence
Developing Mature Interpersonal Relationships • Lack of awareness of differences; intolerance of differences • Intimate relationships are nonexistent, short term, or unhealthy	• Tolerance and appreciation of differences • Intimate partnerships and friendships are enduring and nurturing
Establishing Identity • Discomfort with body, appearance, gender sexuality • Lack of clarity about heritage, or social/cultural background • Confused self-concept • Unclear idea of others' evaluation • Low self-acceptance and self-esteem • Lack of stability and integration	• Comfort with physical self • Clarity about social/cultural roots of identity • Clarity about "who I am" • Awareness of "how others see me" • High self-acceptance and self-esteem • High level of stability and integration

Figure 5.1 Continued	
From	*To*
Developing Integrity	
• Dualistic thinking and rigid beliefs	• Humanizing values
• Unclear or untested personal values and believes	• Personalizing (clarifying and affirming) values while respecting others' beliefs
• Self-interest	• Social responsibility
• Discrepancies between values and actions	• Congruence and authenticity

and Identity, first published in 1969 and then revised in 1993, was aimed at higher education faculty members and administrators but became a manifesto for student affairs practitioners. In updating the seven vectors, Chickering and Reisser (1993) relied heavily on Pascarella and Terenzini's (1991) synthesis of over 2,600 research studies on the impact of college on students, while incorporating more recent research on women, minority groups, gay and lesbian students, and older students. The theory is summarized in Figure 5.1.

Like several earlier influential theories, Chickering's theory was originally based on data gathered in four-year colleges exclusively. In its updated form, however, there is evidence that the theory is broad enough to be relevant to today's community college students, returning adults, and the diverse student bodies found on urban campuses. Several researchers in addition to Pascarella and Terenzini (1991), including Kuh and Wallman (1986) and Graham and Cockriel (1997), have found evidence of changes in directions consistent with Chickering's theory, using broad samples of students from a variety of institutions.

Chickering and Reisser (1993) outline seven key factors that have an impact on development and hypothesize that educationally powerful environments can be created when these factors are put into action:

• *Institutional Objectives:* Institutional objectives need to be clear and taken seriously, and goals and learning outcomes of its diverse programs need to be clear and consistent with these priorities.

• *Institutional Size:* Whether a college is large or small, students need to be actively involved on campus. As the number of persons outstrips the opportunities for significant participation and satisfaction, the developmental potential is reduced. Thus, even if the campus is large, small groups or easily identifiable ways and places to connect with others can help this engagement process.

• *Student-Faculty Relationships:* One of the most consistent findings is that student-faculty interaction is critical for student development, especially when it is frequent and friendly, and occurs in various situations.

• *Curriculum:* An educationally powerful class or learning experience should:
- be relevant to students' backgrounds and prior experiences;
- recognize individual differences;
- expose students to diverse perspectives which challenge pre-existing information, assumptions, and values; and
- provide examples of, opportunities for, and activities that
- help students integrate diverse assumptions and values.

• *Teaching:* Good teaching calls for active learning, encourages student-faculty contact and cooperation among students, gives prompt feedback, emphasizes time spent on tasks and high expectations, and respects diverse talents and ways of knowing.

• *Friendships and student communities:* Development is fostered when students are encouraged to form friendships and to participate in communities that become meaningful subcultures, and when there is diversity of backgrounds and attitudes as well as significant interchanges and shared interests.

• *Student development programs and services:* When student development administrators define themselves as educators working collaboratively with faculty, they increase the direct and indirect impact of programs and services on learning. They can strengthen their respective divisions and institutions by:
- clearly defining core values, mission, and vision;
- maintaining an ethic of quality;
- making people the prime resource;
- learning from the individuals they serve;
- supporting experimentation and innovation;
- orienting toward action;
- analyzing strengths and weaknesses; and
- investing in professional development.

Though the ways in which these factors can be put into operation may take radically different forms in the community college and the traditional four-year institution, they are nonetheless worthy of attention in both.

THEORY INTO PRACTICE
Principles and Examples

To translate theory into practice, several elements must be present. First, key individuals in leadership positions must become familiar enough, and excited about, a particular theory to want to apply it in a focused manner. The more often a chief student affairs officer articulates theoretical principles or raises questions grounded in research, the more likely the theory will be considered. The theories referred to must be perceived as valid and as relevant to the students, to staff needs, and to conditions at the institution. Ideally, a program proposal or research design will incorporate theoretical principles that have been shown to be effective for the population for which the program is designed and should aim at testing a hypothesis. Application of a theory should be linked to current institutional goals wherever possible, and measurement efforts should be coordinated with institutional research offices. Theory application and research findings should then inform follow-up activities and generate further studies.

Core insights can be combined with other theoretical principles and basic management issues during periodic program and system reviews. As an illustration, at Suffolk County Community College's Ammerman Campus, enrollment services staff members have been trying to better serve students who vary in age, interest, and ability. They have been examining ways to balance the value associated with individualized attention with that of enhancing student connections with each other, ways to integrate adult students, members of under-represented groups, and disabled students into a community that balances challenge and support, and ways to increase students' sense of competence in using campus resources and to promote autonomous responsibility for their own financial aid and course planning.

As a result of these efforts, they have experimented with several innovative programs. For example, inquiries are now tracked by a new computer system that generates individual follow-up letters and phone calls. Admissions, Advising and Testing, Financial Aid, Registration, and Cashier's offices now provide services on evenings and Saturdays during peak enrollment periods. New electronic systems for applying for admission and for financial aid are being instituted, and many offices are designing web pages. Child care is offered for infants, toddlers, and pre-schoolers. Students placed into developmental courses receive advisement in individual sessions to maximize support. Other students first meet in a large group event that serves to welcome them to the college and provides instruction in the basics of course selection; they then move to small groups based on intended academic concentration, where they meet with faculty members and other new students with whom they share interests. They learn to find the resources, plan their own class schedules, and register over the telephone. These tasks may seem mundane to those who work with traditional students, but for nontraditional community college students these are achievements.

Peer advisors lead orientation sessions and assist with group advising, thereby gaining valuable skills and confidence. Both group advising and orientation programs are offered in three-hour blocks, in day and evening sessions, enabling working students to choose a time convenient for them and allowing them to move through the process as quickly as possible. Student advisors telephone incoming students after the first two weeks of the semester, encouraging them to join a club, come to the Adult Student Lounge, or attend upcoming special events, many of which are designed for families.

Theory can also infuse greater meaning and focus into student activities, counseling, career services, athletics, multicultural affairs, and other programs that help students to move through the institution or assist them with problems. Chickering's model advocates engaging students in active learning (building competence through practice, experience, feedback, reflection, and modeling), creating learning communities where students from diverse backgrounds can get to know and respect each other, establishing meaningful interaction between students and faculty, supporting students who need extra help, attempting to help students clarify their purposes, and values, to develop a positive sense of self, and to manage problematic impulses and emotions.

Some examples of theory-based programs include:
- competence-based leadership training that teaches planning, budgeting, publicizing, recruitment, and interpersonal skills through simulations and content presentations;
- lectures, concerts, trips, workshops, and special programs planned by students and staff members, which reflect the changing interests of a diverse student body;
- opportunities for hands-on work designing, producing, or performing, as well as sharing creative endeavors, such as poems or artwork;
- effective community-building events that are visible and appealing to campus subgroups, such as African American History Month, Women's Week, Earth Week, an International Festival, Kwanzaa, AIDS Awareness, blood drives, food bank collections, Career Fairs, Health Fairs;
- opportunities for group travel to museums, concerts, conferences, and competitions in other neighborhoods, cities, or countries;
- development of explicit goals for intercollegiate athletics beyond successful competition (such as fostering high grades, teamwork, self-disci-

pline), while providing extra support systems for athletes who need advising, tutoring, study halls, or other kinds of assistance;

• access to the Internet, computers, telecourses, and other forms of individualized or distance learning;

• proactive outreach to at-risk students, through intervention programs, special support programs for low-income, first-generation, or disabled students, or mandatory counseling for students on probation or in danger of losing their financial aid;

• procedures for assuring that all students have a plan of study and a way to match courses taken against degree requirements;

• procedures for dealing promptly with conduct problems, crisis situations, or conflicts in ways that maximize learning to manage emotions and apply ethical judgment;

• well-designed publications that reflect the mission, diversity, and user-friendliness of the institution;

• development of an ethic of care that pervades the institutional culture and affords students an opportunity to talk easily with staff members or peer advisors about their college and life experiences;

• posters, T-shirts, mottos, or symbols that express the culture and values of the institution;

• workshops and other events for helping students clarify long-term goals and locate employment opportunities;

• forums, discussions, or events that focus on current and controversial issues or particular values or cultures;

• advisement systems, club programs, committee structures, and other avenues for bringing students and faculty together; and

• recognition ceremonies, celebrations, and informal gatherings that honor achievement and revitalize community spirit.

Note that these examples are general rather than specific; the specifics emerge from the unique and particular characteristics of the students served.

Theory can also be used to build partnerships with faculty colleagues, and with professionals in schools, other postsecondary institutions, and outside agencies, as well as with community employers. Student affairs practitioners have experience working collaboratively with faculty — in advising students, serving on committees, planning events, awarding scholarships, and assisting students with particular courses. Efforts to promote student development can be enhanced by articulating principles of good practice and applicable theory, and by reinforcing initiatives which improve teaching, curriculum, and student-faculty relationships. For example, student affairs administrators can organize panel discussions on community-building, learning styles, classroom management, or any topic that creates a dialogue that is directly or indirectly related to student development; support colleagues proposing individualized or experiential approaches to learning; provide formal recognition and informal appreciation to faculty who are very effective advisors; and work with administrative counterparts to appoint cochairs of committees, plan campus meetings on issues affecting students, and encourage innovative staff members to apply for grants or establish pilot programs that are consistent with developmental theory.

Strong ties to community employers have spurred the creation of new training programs that are responsive to the needs of a changing marketplace, and which involve students in competence-based learning. For example, Suffolk County Community College is forming partnerships with emerging industries and local high schools to create seamless work-based learning opportunities. Five growth industries have been targeted: emerging electronic technologies, graphic communications, medical imaging and health care information systems, biotechnology and bioengineering, and computer software. Industry leaders and educators are revising curricula and designing training programs that can be tailored to the needs of working adults and that can help produce a technologically sophisticated workforce.

These changes have profound implications for higher education. According to Hahn (1997), up to 75 percent of the current workforce will require retraining within the next ten years, and more than half of all new jobs will require postsecondary education. In addition, 82 percent of the new entrants to the workforce by the year 2000 will be women and minorities. Adults, the majority of them female, are returning to college in greater numbers and are looking for up-to-date technology, customer service, child care, evening and weekend courses and services, and the possibility of completing a degree on a part-time basis. Above all, they want to acquire the competence and knowledge needed for career success. Yet many postsecondary institutions remain entrenched in outdated approaches that do not provide enough flexibility or train students with relevant skills. A recent study from the Business-Higher Education Forum (American Council on Education, 1997) underscores this point:

> While new hires said the education they received gave them "impressive academic skill" and corporate leaders believe that "today's graduates are at least as good as their predecessors and perhaps better," neither "is entirely satisfied with the transition of students from campus to workplace." Corporate leaders believe recent graduates lack qualifications in many areas, including communication skills, ability to work in teams, the ability to work with people from diverse backgrounds and adequate ethics training (p. 1).

Just as more community colleges are working closely with high schools to provide early assessment of math, reading, and writing skills, and conducting on-site admissions appointments, four-year colleges and universities can more intentionally create bridges to community colleges as will be discussed in greater detail in Chapter Six. More person-to-person exchanges would bring about a dialogue among colleagues — academic departments and student services personnel — who can share their front line experiences with transfer students. Too often, however, staff members at institutions located within miles of each other do not interact. Given their ability to organize, student affairs administrators could play key roles in coordinating intercampus meetings or small conferences.

The Washington Center for the Improvement of Undergraduate Education, based at the Evergreen State University, has done an exemplary job catalyzing coordinated study options at both two-year and four-year institutions, primarily by inviting interested parties to look at models and share ideas. As a result, interdisciplinary teams, Freshman Interest Groups, and other types of learning communities have proliferated throughout the state of Washington. A conference on "Work in the Next Decade," hosted by a community college, led to expanded on-the-job learning opportunities through cooperative education, internships, and independent study. Four-year institutions also need to reach beyond their campuses by creating more ways for students to volunteer, study abroad, or visit experts in their field. Like community colleges, four-year institutions must create a warm climate for diversity, a welcoming array of options for adult and part-time students, and provide myriad ways for students to bond with each other.

RESEARCH AGENDA

As hard as it may be, student affairs practitioners need to review current research and to initiate data-gathering efforts. Information is needed about the impact of college on student satisfaction, achievement, success, and development. We need feedback from students in order to improve programs and services and to meet accountability or accreditation standards. A first step is to clarify the goals of specific programs or the desired developmental outcomes for students in general. Then, a method for gathering data can be designed, ideally in consultation with the campus office for institutional research. An ambitious research agenda might include a variety of approaches, such as:

- gathering data on incoming students' characteristics and goals, as part of the placement testing process, by sampling freshman seminar partici-

pants, or by participating in national studies;
- surveying users of specific services or participants in specific programs;
- comparing program participants with nonparticipants to identify differing levels of performance or development, using pre- and post-tests, surveys, observations, interviews, and self-assessments;
- gathering qualitative information by organizing focus groups, observing programs, or interviewing current students;
- surveying or interviewing students withdrawing from the college to ascertain their reasons and future plans, as well as the level of their satisfaction with services and the impact of programs;
- assessing graduating students' perceptions of the impact of college on their lives;
- assessing alumni in terms of their further education, employment, and other developmental outcomes;
- conducting studies comparing continuing students and those who withdraw or a comparable population who did not attend college;
- conducting longitudinal studies of a cohort group as it proceeds through college and beyond.

Information from the community and from other institutions also needs to be gathered. Market research can ascertain the changing needs of potential students and the perceptions of parents and employers about the effectiveness of college programs and services. Community colleges need to assess the transfer process and its academic and developmental impact on students and to get information about how its graduates' performance compares with students who begin at four-year institutions. The colleges in turn need to provide information to high schools about their graduates and their preparedness for college work. Employers who hire graduates should be surveyed to ascertain whether the graduates have needed skills.

Research is needed to test and revise emerging theories. For example, more studies must be conducted on the interactions between age, race, gender, sexual orientation, culture, and student development. Typological theories have identified the various learning styles and personality traits that affect individual responses to environmental challenges, and it is important to determine the extent to which divergent theories must be applied for different subgroups or different cultures . While no single theory can apply to all the many human characteristics, valuable theories are characterized by logical coherence, usefulness, and a generalizability that allows them to be applied to various populations and settings. We need research that can make broad theories more inclusive rather than focusing too narrowly on group-specific models. The conceptual frameworks that have been put forth must be tested, refined through application, and revised through successive cycles of informed practice and empirical research. Theory and practice are inextricable. Practitioners must also be on the lookout for useful theories that do not appear in student affairs journals, but which may be found in the publications of social science, business, or other education-related disciplines.

CONCLUSION

Community college practitioners have often been hands-on pragmatists and generalists. Having been asked to serve the broadest array of students, with small classes and low tuition rates, they have been attuned to what works best to promote student success. Collectively, they have much experience in adapting programs to serve women, part-timers, students of color, disabled students, and those requiring remedial work. They have supported honors students and international students. They have counseled ex-convicts, mental patients, and parents on public assistance. They have tailored their programs to adults taking a single course, laid-off workers seeking retraining, and seniors looking for personal enrichment. Inherent in this responsiveness is a commitment to individualizing and personalizing the educational process, whenever possible, and to adapting systems to accommodate student needs while still holding high expectations that students meet the institution's standards.

As the examples in this chapter have illustrated, theory and research can help institutions adapt and revitalize. The impetus to adapt may be precipitated by an impending accreditation visit, enrollment decline, or state mandate to assess outcomes. Ideally, it should be part of an ongoing attempt to experiment, evaluate, and refine. Without theory, research, and a commitment to improve practice, both two-year and four-year institutions may continue to simply count numbers of students served rather than gauging the impact of services on student development.

There are numerous ways community college practitioners have applied theory effectively or have incorporated principles into institutional mission statements or departmental goals. Those working in four-year institutions have much to gain from a dialogue with their colleagues in two-year schools who have been out on the front lines for years. Yet there are few forums for comparing notes. Perhaps it is time to take the initiative in organizing dialogues between two- and four-year institutions. Graduate faculty and students carrying out research in higher education would be natural participants, as would community college graduates who have transferred to four-year institutions. Such discussions could use theory as context for discussions about student-centered learning, community-building, academic and social integration, or identity development within a multicultural society.

Leaders at four-year and two-year institutions need to extend the discussion beyond improving services or understanding student characteristics by asking more basic questions. For example, what are the most important outcomes and how do we measure added value? Is there a gap between why students are coming to college and what colleges actually offer to them? How are students from different racial backgrounds interacting and learning from each other? How well are students being prepared for work in the next century? How are the faculty advising students, and how do students view their relationships with faculty advisors? How are the student affairs offices adapting to the changing needs of students? How are students encouraged to become more socially responsible and ethical?

One of the ironies of working in higher education is that practitioners rarely take the time to talk about teaching and learning or theory and practice. Yet undergraduate education is in need of revitalization, and much of the theory needed to reform it is already in place. The challenge is to apply it while remaining in close contact with our varied customers, to assess each student's needs and abilities using our theoretical lenses, and to offer powerful ways to increase intellectual and interpersonal competence, clarify purposes and values, form meaningful relationships, and develop a sense of self as a caring and confident citizen of the world.

References

American Council on Education. (1997). Spanning the chasm: Corporate and academic cooperation to improve work-force preparation. *On Campus*. [Online serial]. Available at http://www.aft.org.

Chickering, A. W., & Reisser, L. (1993). *Education and identity*. (2nd Ed.). San Francisco: Jossey-Bass.

Graham, S., & Cockriel, I. (1997). A factor structure for social and personal development outcomes in college. *Journal of College Student Development, 34*, 199-216.

Hahn, C. (June 16, 1997). Education for the region's future. *Long Island*, 16-17.

Kuh, G. D., & Wallman, G. H. (1986). Outcomes oriented marketing. In D. Hossler (Ed.), *Managing college enrollments*. (New Directions for Higher Education, No. 53) (pp. 63-72). San Francisco: Jossey-Bass.

Pascarella, E., & Terenzini, P. (1991). *How college affects students: Findings and insights from twenty years of research*. San Francisco: Jossey-Bass.

Upcraft. M. L. (1993). Translating theory into practice. In M. J. Barr and associates, *The handbook of student affairs administration* (pp. 260-273). San Francisco: Jossey-Bass.

CHAPTER FOUR

Infiltrating Academe

by Marguerite M. Culp

"*T*he notion of a single institution with distinct, immutable departments within which faculty and staff members perform well-defined roles is a tired idea whose time is past" contend Alfred and Carter (1997, p. 41). Their sentiments are shared by student affairs practitioners (Culp & Helfgot, 1995; Kuh, 1996) as well as educational leaders with little or no formal connection to student affairs (Boggs, 1995; Hutchings, 1996; Lorenzo & LeCroy, 1994).

One of the common convictions of community college student affairs practitioners is a belief that divisions do in fact divide, and that the existence of a student affairs division does not mean that it should remain within its own domain, confining its programs to its traditional areas of responsibility. In fact, partnerships that benefit the institution and increase the probability that its students will succeed are central to the fulfillment of the missions of these departments, because the communities the institutions serve demand both access and excellence and the businesses with whom they work have little patience with or respect for a divided academic world. Studying the strategies of infiltrating academe used by community college colleagues can help student affairs practitioners in colleges and universities establish connections with the faculty, create partnerships that benefit students, and increase their prospects of surviving in circumstances of intense competition for limited economic resources.

MINDING EVERYONE'S BUSINESS
Student Affairs in the Community College

In many respects, successful student affairs practitioners in community colleges have always minded everyone else's business: they collected data to help academic colleagues identify demographic trends and student needs; they worked with the faculty, the staff, students, and community members to create programs and services that increase the probability of student success; and they learned about all aspects of campus life — instruction, business, administration — to identify opportunities and challenges for student affairs. Sometimes student affairs practitioners had central roles in their interactions with other campus groups, and other times they played supporting or consulting roles. Most of the time, however, these practitioners served as brokers who brought together various groups to create partnerships that benefitted students and the faculty who taught them.

Currently, student affairs administrators in colleges and universities are discussing the need to create partnerships between student affairs and academic affairs to control costs, increase institutional effectiveness, and create seamless learning environments for students (Kuh, 1996). *The Student Learning Imperative: Implications for Student Affairs* (American College Personnel Association, 1994) ignited a national debate in the profession when it challenged practitioners to examine the role of student affairs and to redirect resources to support the teaching-learning process. *Reform in Student Affairs* (Bloland, Stamatakos & Rogers, 1994) added fuel to the fire by declaring the student development movement a failure and challenging student affairs practitioners to connect more with the academic community and "to reach out aggressively to involve teaching faculty in programs and activities" (p. 109).

Student affairs practitioners in community colleges preceded their college and university colleagues in understanding that one of the keys to student success is found in the relationship that exists between the student affairs and academic affairs staffs. Community college practitioners also understood the need to connect programs and services to their institution's educational mission and to define their relationship with the faculty as a partnership, albeit one often difficult to establish and a challenge to maintain (Culp & Helfgot, 1995), but still one that, when it works, benefits the students, the faculty, and the institution in three ways.

Partnerships Help Faculty Succeed

Student affairs practitioners in community colleges have long understood that faculty were subject-matter specialists who knew a great deal about a specific academic area but very little about the students with whom they hoped to share their knowledge. They shared O'Banion's (1994) perception that community college faculty members, particularly those hired in the early period of the development of community colleges, were not "schooled in adult development theory or basic theories of learning," had "little or no experience in working with the diversity of students flocking to these new opportunities for higher education," and carried "heavy teaching loads while also serving as academic advisors, participating on numerous committees, and sponsoring various student organizations" (1994, p. 20). By sharing their knowledge of adult development theory, assessment and testing strategies, classroom management techniques, learning and teaching styles, outcomes assessment procedures, and research and statistics, student affairs staff members have created partnerships with faculty that married theory and practice and made it more likely that faculty members would be able to understand and teach the very diverse students who were pouring into community college classrooms through the open door.

Partnerships Encourage the Institution to
Fulfill its Mission

Almost from their inception, community colleges served the most challenging of all students in higher education: at-risk adults who were underprepared, worked 30 or more hours a week, were the first in their families to attend college, and had "failure expectations" (Roueche & Roueche, 1993, p. 1). They also served some of the best prepared students: high school honors graduates unable to leave home to attend a university, mature learners prepared to do what it took to earn a degree, and talented midlife career changers excited about and prepared to acquire the education that would allow them to succeed in their efforts to shift vocational direction. Because at-risk students presented unique challenges in the classroom, many campus and community groups questioned whether community colleges should even attempt to serve them, particularly as the pressure has increased to improve graduation and retention figures, reduce loan default rates, and improve performance on licensing exams. By working with faculty and staff members to increase their comfort and skill levels with at-risk students, student affairs staff members have increased the probability that their institutions would remain faithful to their mission and serve all of the community, not just those members who were easy to understand and teach. By working with students to improve their ability to benefit from instruction, student affairs practitioners have increased the prospect that these students would succeed and that faculty would view them as capable of learning at the college level.

Partnerships Reduce the Odds that
Differences Become Deficits

Roueche and Roueche (1993) observed that "the at-risk student is becoming the new majority" (p. vii); "the public education system is not delivering a literate and well informed student/product" (p. 6); and "many individuals have ceased to believe in education as a path to a better life" (p. 15). Since most of the at-risk, poorly prepared students with unclear career goals and marginal study skills entered higher education through the community college, the faculty and staff members of these institutions have faced challenges unheard of in colleges and universities. Without adequate services — assessment and course placement, proactive pre-enrollment orientation, intrusive career counseling, developmental advising, academic early warning and student tracking systems, and planned support services that extended from acceptance through graduation — differences would have become deficits for a large percentage of at-risk community college students. By working with faculty and staff members to create structure and support for at-risk students, community college student affairs practitioners have decreased the chance that differences would push students through the revolving door into lives of poverty. By establishing partnerships with faculty and staff members to work with local public school systems, student affairs personnel have increased the likelihood that future students would come to the community college prepared to benefit from higher education.

BREAKING DOWN BARRIERS

In "The Yin & Yang of Student Learning in College," Elizabeth Blake (1996), former vice-chancellor for academic affairs at the University of Minnesota and a strong advocate for academic and student affairs partnerships, identifies four differences between student affairs and academic personnel:

- Student affairs work tends to attract people whose personality contrasts sharply with those of typical faculty members.

- The nature of learning that occurs in areas of concern to student affairs staff members contrasts in fundamental ways with the learning that takes place in college coursework.
- Faculty and student affairs departments may be seeking to realize very different, perhaps incompatible, outcomes even though they work with the same students.
- At times, both the faculty and the student affairs staff feel put down by each other.

Although Blake's experiences were in a large university, most community college practitioners would agree that community college faculty members and student affairs practitioners often have very different perspectives on the academic world, perspectives that everyone needs to examine if colleges are to succeed in the task of teaching students whose backgrounds differ significantly from those of the faculty and staff members. Given these differences and the fact that most faculty members see little need for creating partnerships with one another much less with their colleagues in student affairs, how can student affairs practitioners infiltrate academe to the point that faculty will even begin to discuss forming partnerships? Analyzing the strategies that have been used by community college practitioners over the years will help student affairs professionals in colleges and universities provide stronger support for students and faculty. Examining the products of these partnerships and understanding how they increased the probability of student success will encourage college and university student affairs practitioners to risk breaking down the barriers that exist in their institutions.

Create Shared Philosophy, Goals, and Objectives

A student affairs department with a coherent philosophy, premised on the assumption that student affairs exists both to support the teaching-learning process and to increase the probability of student success, may be able to establish a cooperative relation with the faculty simply by meeting with members of each academic department and discussing the mission of student affairs, the year's goals and objectives, and how these goals and objectives should inform programs and activities. Most of the time, however, creating shared philosophy, goals, and objectives involves much work, which can be divided into three phases.

- *Establishing a Baseline.* What do faculty members know about and expect from student affairs? There are many ways to gather this information but the three most effective strategies seem to be *focus groups*, *needs analysis surveys*, and the *Modified Delphi Technique*. Using the *focus group* approach, student affairs practitioners ask faculty members to meet with a facilitator in groups of between eight to twelve participants to respond to a series of questions about student affairs. Faculty members may be randomly assigned to groups or each group may be composed of faculty members from the same academic area. The facilitator asks the same questions of each group, records the responses, and prepares a report for the student affairs office. Student affairs practitioners analyze the facilitator's report to identify faculty perceptions of the role that student affairs currently plays in the life of the institution, the program's contribution to the institution's bottom line, and the role that student affairs needs to play in the future.

• Although not as personal as the focus group approach, the *needs analysis survey* can produce valuable data if carefully constructed. Usually a one-page document, the needs analysis survey asks faculty members to indicate which of the services currently provided by student affairs are essential to the mission of the college, which are important but not essential, and which could be eliminated without affecting the institution's mission. The survey also asks faculty members to use the same criteria to evaluate services that the student affairs department might provide in the future.

• In the *Modified Delphi* approach, faculty members receive a list of the programs and services currently provided by student affairs practitioners and are asked to select five (or ten, or fifteen) that are the most essential to the institution's mission. Faculty responses are collated, services receiving no or very few votes are eliminated; faculty members again are asked to select their top five, this time also being asked to indicate *why* they chose each program or service. Again, responses are tabulated, programs and services with no votes are eliminated, and the list, accompanied by the reasons for each selection, is returned to the faculty. The process continues until faculty members reach consensus on the five, ten, or fifteen student affairs programs or services that are essential to the institution's mission.

Build Shared Definitions

All three approaches — the focus group, the needs analysis survey, and the Modified Delphi technique — provide a foundation for a dialogue that must take place if student affairs practitioners are to redefine their philosophy, goals, and objectives in terms of the institution's overall objectives. These investigations also provide a snapshot of faculty perceptions of student affairs departments at a specific point in time, identify areas where faculty do not have accurate data, and demonstrate the areas where student affairs staff members must begin their efforts to break down barriers, create shared definitions, and develop productive faculty/student affairs partnerships. To fulfill these beginnings — to achieve shared definitions and productive partnerships — student affairs staff members must provide the faculty with data to correct inaccurate perceptions, meet with faculty members individually and in groups to share information about the outcomes of programs and services, and, in general, constantly work to maintain communication with faculty colleagues.

Give Faculty a Stake in Student Services

Even at the community colleges considered the best, faculty members need constant reinforcement, continual reminders of the methods, aims, and perspectives of the student affairs staff, ongoing evidence that the student affairs department contributes to the institution's mission. One of the most effective ways to bind faculty members to the student affairs department is by establishing joint screening, tenure, and advisory committees; establishing cross-functional teams to solve specific problems, create new programs, or evaluate existing modes of operation; and by including faculty representatives in annual operational and strategic planning sessions.

Many faculty members, however, have neither the time nor the interest to serve on student affairs committees. Practitioners can give such faculty members a stake in student affairs through formal and informal communications with them throughout the year by, for example, sending weekly e-mail messages; preparing monthly newsletters and distributing staff meeting minutes; holding annual town meetings; appointing a student affairs liaison to major divisions or departments; appointing an administrative liaison to the Faculty Senate; appointing student affairs personnel to major campus committees; establishing a welcome wagon program that assigns new full-time faculty to a student affairs staff member who makes sure that the faculty member understands the mission of student affairs; establishing a student affairs "hotline" that faculty members can use to report problems or share concerns; placing suggestion boxes in faculty office areas; scheduling monthly "Dine with the Dean" brown-bag lunches in which faculty meet with the dean of students to discuss strategies to improve student affairs by 1 percent per month; and establishing paid summer internships for faculty members in the student affairs office.

CREATE LINKAGES WITH ACADEMIC AFFAIRS

While community college supporters "like to talk romantically about the educational virtues of having such a diversity of students in the classroom, in reality it is difficult to create anything resembling a 'peer group' out of such a hodge-podge of students" (Astin, 1993, p. 416). This inability to create peer groups coupled with the challenges of teaching so many different types of students, many of whom are academically unprepared and lacking clear career direction, often translates into high drop-out rates for which faculty are held responsible. The desire of the faculty to reduce drop-out rates and increase retention and graduation rates without compromising academic standards provides fertile ground for faculty/student affairs partnerships.

Help Faculty Market Their Academic Fields

Shifting enrollment patterns concern faculty members, whose jobs depend on students deciding to take their classes. Student affairs staff members can help faculty recruit outside of the institution by: inviting area high schools to hold their "College Nights" on the community college campus; scheduling career fairs on the campus and at area high schools; arranging for faculty to participate in "Teach-Ins" at area elementary, middle, and high schools; and offering workshops for high school teachers and counselors taught by community college faculty. Student affairs staffs, particularly those involved in student activities, can help faculty change the image of the community college in the high schools by inviting high school students to co- and extracurricular activities on the campus, facilitating leadership retreats and training sessions for officers of high school organizations, and sponsoring seminars on a variety of topics of interest to high school students. The process of helping undecided community college students to select a major provides almost unlimited collaborative opportunities for academic and student affairs practitioners. Guest appearances in Life/Career Planning classes, workshops entitled "What to do with a major in . . .", career fairs for on-campus students, and career centers organized around the programs available at the college are a few of the strategies used by community college student affairs practitioners to help students select a major *and* provide faculty members with opportunities to talk about their academic areas.

Improve Students' Readiness to Learn

Community college faculty members are interested in improving the performance of currently enrolled students and in increasing the quality of the academic pool from which the college will draw future students. An orientation program that teaches students how to succeed in college is the first step to improving the performance of new students. Such a program may last two hours, two days, or an entire semester, but it provides students with a realistic picture of the skills, time, and effort required to succeed and forces them to make realistic decisions about the type and number of courses to take and the support services they will need during their first semester.

Many community colleges offer companion orientation sessions for the families of new students so they will be able to understand, anticipate the needs of, and support their sons, daughters, spouses, parents, and friends as they deal with the demands of college. Faculty members participate in these orientation sessions in a variety of ways: preparing three-to-five minute videos describing their class and teaching style, leading small group discussions, appearing in an orientation video, advising students and their parents, teaching all or part of an orientation course. This participation provides the foundation for future faculty/student affairs/student partnerships. This cooperative venture continues into the student's first semester, as faculty and student affairs staff members collaborate to teach College Success courses for at-risk students; offer seminars designed to improve participants' ability to study, listen, take notes, manage time, take tests, and deal with test anxiety; and incorporate units on study and test taking skills into existing academic classes.

One of the most important faculty/student affairs partnerships is the one designed to help the college identify students in danger of failing or dropping out early in the semester. Almost every community college in the country has an early warning system in place that encourages, or sometimes requires, faculty members to refer students who miss class, fall behind in their outside assignments, or fail quizzes to the student affairs staff members who work with the student to identify options and connect them with support services. Finally, student affairs personnel build a reservoir of good will with faculty by organizing support groups for students on probation or seeking readmission after suspension.

The prospect of increasing the likelihood that future students will enter the community college more academically prepared than currently enrolled students provides unique opportunities to infiltrate the academic sections of the university. Many community colleges sponsor summer camps for at-risk juniors that help students increase their ability to read, write, calculate, compute, study, and take tests. Others work with high school counselors to identify at-risk graduating seniors, encourage these students to apply early, and provide developmental courses over the summer to better prepare them for the academic classes they will take during their first semester.

The experiences of the student services office at Seminole Community College in Sanford, Florida, from 1988 to 1996, demonstrate how partnerships provide win-win outcomes. To increase the likelihood that new students would succeed, counselors worked with the faculty to develop and produce an orientation video entitled "How to Succeed at SCC"; implemented a mandatory two-to-three-hour orientation program that involved faculty, staff members, and students; asked students to complete a 50-question New Student Survey, the results of which were used to develop a profile of the entering class, identify at-risk students, and connect students to programs, services, and organizations; and developed educational and support-service plans for all new college credit students. During the last hectic week of registration and the first week of classes, faculty worked at help stations at strategic campus locations to provide new students with information and directions and to act as troubleshooters for registration-related problems, thus freeing student affairs staff members to advise, assess, orient, and register.

During the students' first semester, counselors collaborated with faculty to teach College Success, a two-credit course based on David Ellis' (1985) *Becoming a Master Student*; used New Student Survey results to identify at-risk students, and offered units on study skills, test-taking skills, test anxiety, time management, and learning styles as part of an existing credit class or after class for extra credit; implemented an academic early warning system; and collaborated with faculty to create cocurricular student activities that were an extension of the classroom and that helped develop a sense of community at the college. Counselors also included faculty as guest speakers or panel members in their three-credit Life-Career Planning courses and as presenters in the New Directions Program, both of which were designed to help undecided students select a major and increase the probability that they would remain in college.

To better prepare middle and high school students for Seminole Community College, the student services office established several unique partnerships with the Seminole County Public Schools. The 2+2+2 Program brought together K-12, community college, and university faculty members to create seamless curricula in a variety of academic areas. Through the Computerized Placement Testing Program, the community college offered to test high school sophomores to calculate their chances of entering college without the need for developmental courses and to identify academic weakness in time for the Seminole County Public Schools to better prepare them for college. A grant-funded summer Career Counseling Institute for middle and elementary counselors enhanced the ability of public school counselors to establish career counseling programs, link these programs to the community college and the world of work, and have access to the resources of Seminole Community College's Career/Placement Center. Another grant-funded project, the Tech Prep Institute, offered Seminole County teachers, parents, and counselors an opportunity to understand the importance of career counseling, explore the Tech Prep opportunities available at the college, and interact with college faculty and staff members. In partnership with the Seminole Community College faculty, the student services office produces the *High School Advising Manual* every year to help middle and high school counselors assist students to select the courses that would prepare them to enter the community college without having to register for remedial courses, and hosted the Annual Counselor Workshop, an event that brought central Florida educational and agency counselors to the campus for a day.

Increase Faculty Members' Ability to Reach and Teach

Even dedicated faculty members who want to do a good job and help their students to succeed feel challenged by the ever-changing student body at community colleges. The faculty member's desire to be effective in the classroom presents student affairs practitioners with opportunities to help him or her understand, anticipate the needs of, and adapt to successive waves of new students.

Community college admissions offices routinely collect data on new students; registrars study enrollment patterns; financial aid officers predict financial need; and counselors understand the collective personality of an entering class sooner than anyone else on campus. When the information collected by these four offices is collated, analyzed, compared to data from previous years, and packaged in an understandable form, it provides faculty members with a snapshot of the new students, an understanding of how these students compare to and differ from previous students, and a reference point that can be used to initiate a dialogue concerning how to reach and teach these particular students. Many community colleges break down information about new students by divisions and departments to increase the likelihood that faculty will identify with the data and actually use it to change the way they teach.

Whether they teach in small community colleges or large universities, most faculty members enter the profession because they love their field and want to share this love with others. As a result, faculty are subject-matter rich, student-knowledge poor and, in an era of declining enrollments and an emphasis on retention, eager to broaden their ability to understand and teach students from diverse backgrounds. As colleagues who have spent much of their professional lives studying adult development, assessment, learning and teaching styles, classroom management, and research and statistics, student affairs practitioners have much to give their faculty peers and can offer to share this knowledge in a variety of formal and informal settings. Again, some of the programs created between 1988 and 1996 by faculty and student affairs colleagues at Seminole Community College exemplify the productive faculty/student affairs partnerships that exist at many two-year colleges.

Brainstorming Sessions
During August planning days in 1996, over 150 faculty and staff members participated in three-hour small group brainstorming sessions to identify classroom strategies that have the potential to increase the prospects for students academic success. In collaboration with the Retention Committee, the student services office collated suggestions from the brainstorming sessions, published them as *151 Strategies to Increase the Chances that Students Will Succeed at SCC,* and distributed copies of the document to all full-time and adjunct faculty.

Coffee and Conversation
To follow-up on the momentum of the August brainstorming sessions, the Retention Committee, in conjunction with the student services office, hosted a standing-room only Coffee and Conversation in April to enable faculty members to evaluate the effectiveness of suggested retention strategies, share information about additional strategies formulated during the year, and identify issues for future meetings. Again, over 150 faculty and staff members participated, and the student services office published volume II of *Retention Strategies that Work at SCC*.

Counselor Workshops for Faculty
Each year, counselors offered a variety of workshops that faculty could incorporate into their classes, offer for extra credit, or include in a regu-

larly scheduled faculty meeting. Outlined in an attractive brochure that was mailed to all full-time and adjunct faculty, these workshops covered a range of topics from AIDS awareness and sex education to learning styles, study and test taking skills, time management, and celebrating diversity. Twelve to fifteen topics were offered each year: a core group of topics supplemented by additional subjects added on the basis of counselor skills and faculty needs.

Faculty Forums
During the academic year, the student services office sponsored three Faculty Forums. Coordinated by a member of the Counseling Department, the forums brought faculty and counselors together with an outside consultant to learn about and brainstorm about solutions to shared challenges. The topics in 1996-97 included identifying and dealing with students with disabilities, classroom management techniques, and increasing the chances that students will transfer with minimal loss of credit.

Learning and Teaching Style Workshops
Each year, the student services office offered a series of Myers-Briggs based workshops to help faculty identify their personality type and teaching style, understand the learning styles of their students, and develop strategies to teach students whose learning styles were incompatible with their teaching styles. Between 1988 and 1996, almost half of the full-time faculty participated in workshops which produced three resources used extensively at the college — a study skills method for each of the 16 learning styles, an analysis of the 16 different learning styles and their implications for teaching, an analysis of 16 different teaching styles and the impact of each on the student's ability to learn — as well as companion workshops for students, many of which were offered as part of for-credit classes.

Placement Model
Assessment and Testing Center staff members worked closely with the faculty to develop realistic models to guide the placement of students in all courses, but particularly in the areas of English, mathematics, and reading. Once implemented, these models were tested continually to verify their effectiveness, identify problems, and improve initial course placement. Using these models, counselors worked to place students in appropriate classes and worked with faculty to identify and institute realistic pre- and

co-requisites for courses. From the faculty member's perspective, this was one of the most important instruction/student affairs partnerships, since it increased the probability that the students in his or her classroom were able to benefit from instruction. Student affairs practitioners also viewed this as a critical partnership because it provided them with an opportunity to explicitly raise the ongoing debate about the role of entrance require-ments, cutoff scores, and prerequisites in the life of a community college.

Position Papers

The student services office researched specific topics and published posi-tion papers for the college community. One of the most useful position papers was the *Annual Profile of New Students,* which provided demo-graphic information about new students, analyzed the students' strengths and weaknesses, and identified major student trends and patterns. Other briefer position papers dealt with identifying and meeting the needs of students with attention deficit disorder, defining the role of faculty in the disciplinary process, coping with the disruptive student, and identifying and referring the suicidal student.

Research

Faculty members need to know a great deal more about the students they serve, the effectiveness of the services they provide, and the impact of specific teaching strategies on the institution's bottom line, i.e., student success. They also need to be reassured that money spent on student ser-vices is money well spent. Although much of the research related to these issues should be conducted by the Institutional Research Office, in most community colleges this office is overworked, understaffed, and strangled by state-mandated reporting requirements. To bridge the gap at Seminole Community College, the student activities office, the counseling depart-ment, and the data center teamed up with faculty to conduct several simple but effective retention studies, the results of which provided realistic pic-tures of why students withdrew from classes, why they did not return to college after completing a term, and what their perceptions of the institu-tion were. Research results were published and used to guide campus-wide retention conversations. The student services office also worked with the faculty to identify research topics in student services — How effective was advising for students of color? Did the Life/Career Planning classes make a difference? Were the College Success classes effective? —designed research studies to explore those topics, published the results, and used those results to refine programs and services.

Retention Institute

The student services office successfully collaborated with the College Retention Committee to write a grant to create the Retention Institute, where faculty members could come together to learn about and share insight into good teaching practices, to interact with experts in the field, and to keep their skills on the leading edge of techniques for community college instruction.

Tracking System for At-Risk Students

Using New Student Survey results, the student services office identified the 250 most at-risk new students, received permission from these students to track their academic progress, and implemented a simple Early Warning System. Every two weeks, faculty members received a computer print-out with the name and social security number of the at-risk students enrolled in each of their course sections. Faculty members were asked to answer three questions concerning each student: a) was his or her attendance up-to-date? b) was his or her work up-to-date? c) was the student's current grade at least a "C"? The data center processed the faculty sheets and generated a list of the students whose attendance or work was not up-to-date or who were in danger of failing the course. Counselors or peer partners conferred with these students about their academic status, developed plans to help the students improve their performance, referred them to on- and off-campus support services, and monitored their progress for the rest of the semester. Over 90 percent of the faculty who were asked to provide feedback on the 250 at-risk students did so within 72 hours. Each of these cooperative ventures increased faculty members' ability to reach and teach all students, particularly those identified as at-risk, and provided concrete evidence that student affairs practitioners were partners in the teaching-learning process.

Create Effective Advising Programs

Community college faculty members value effective advising above everything else. If student affairs practitioners cannot advise effectively, they will never have the opportunity to create partnerships with faculty members who may refuse to work with practitioners who, in their opinion, have failed to fulfill their institutional responsibility, i.e., making certain that students register for the right courses. Since many student affairs practitioners, particularly those who function as counselors, do not view advising as their main mission, they often mistakingly divest themselves of that responsibility or undertake advisement as an afterthought. No matter who advises students — counselors, faculty members, professional advisors, or a combination of all three — effective student affairs programs must support the advising process and use it to create linkages with instruction. Advising manuals developed in cooperation with faculty in each academic area offer an excellent place to start. Published in loose-leaf notebooks and distributed to advisors, counselors, and faculty members, these manuals also are at the college's web site and will eventually become the foundation of an electronic degree audit system. Electronic Degree Audit Systems free advisors from counting credits, encourage students to take responsibility for tracking their academic progress, and decrease the possibility that advising errors will occur. The creation and maintenance of such systems provide natural linkages between academic and student affairs. Few graduate students preparing to teach at the college level take classes entitled How to Advise Developmentally, but faculty and student affairs staff members need to sharpen their skills in this area. In advising workshops, faculty members can share with student affairs personnel their knowledge about course content and difficulty, the correct sequencing of courses, and future curriculum changes. Student affairs practitioners can teach faculty members about the needs of the adult student, upper division transfer requirements, how to help students balance the demands of college with the demands of day-to-day life, and the emerging job market.

Community colleges do not operate in a vacuum. Their graduates must be able to transfer with minimal loss of credit to a college or university, or enter business and industry with useful skills. Both the transfer and job placement functions provide student affairs departments with opportunities to create important faculty partnerships. Working together to support the transfer function, faculty members and student affairs staff members can negotiate and monitor articulation agreements with colleges and universities, agreements that identify the courses the upper division institution will accept and the criteria community college students must meet to be admitted. At Seminole Community College, faculty and student affairs staff members not only negotiated articulation agreements but also collaborated on the publication of *Transfer Tips*, a quarterly newsletter for transfer students, and *Opening Doors*, a manual designed to guide prospective graduates through the transfer process and into the university; hosted articulation workshops with local colleges and universities, both public and private, to identify and solve articulation challenges; and created Co-Advisement, an award-winning program in which college faculty members and counselors joined university faculty members in a team that cooperatively advised transfer students.

To support the job placement function, student affairs staff members can work with faculty members to make certain that students master basic résumé writing and interviewing techniques, participate in practice interviews with videotaped feedback, and know how to search for a job. Community colleges with Career/Placement Centers can cooperate even more with faculty by creating job banks, acting as liaisons with local employers to develop job opportunities for students, and tracking who gets jobs.

Teach Courses

Faculty members respect those who teach and those who learn. Student affairs staff members who teach — and teach well — have numerous opportunities to create linkages with faculty colleagues. Some community colleges encourage student affairs staff members to teach as adjuncts in various academic departments: the registrar with an MBA teaches Introduction to Business, the dean with an MA in Psychology teaches Human Growth and Development, and the counselor with a BS in Mathematics teaches Basic Algebra.

Other community colleges include teaching as part of the staff member's job description. Based on their qualifications, student affairs staff members teach College Success, Developmental Psychology, Life/Career Planning, Orientation, or Study Skills. Whether teaching is optional or required, student affairs staff members use their teaching connections to build bridges to the academic world, to participate in department staff meetings, and to solicit teaching tips from faculty. Student affairs staff members also find that teaching raises their awareness level of the real world of the faculty: the life cycle of a class, the difficulty of teaching the unprepared and the unmotivated, and the need to respond to the continual (and often conflicting) demands of the chief academic officer, the chief business officer, the chief student affairs officer, the state Department of Education, and various regulatory agencies.

Share Student Success Stories

Everyone loves a winner, but immersed in a battle to provide a postsecondary education to an unprecedented number of often badly prepared students, many of whom are members of historically under-represented populations, the system within which the faculty functions tends to focus on those who fail. Legislators are not satisfied with completion rates; special interest groups hold faculty responsible for low retention figures; college and university faculty attack their community college counterparts for inadequately preparing transfer students; and board members want to know the percentage of students who fail courses. By reminding faculty of their successes, student affairs staff members send a clear message that they identify with and value the struggles of their faculty colleagues. By sponsoring programs that help faculty members retain students, meet with college and university peers to identify and resolve transfer issues, and improve their course completion rates, student affairs staff members signal that they are partners, not spectators, in the battle to educate students. Many strategies that help faculty recognize and celebrate their successes already have been identified in this chapter, but two additional ones should be mentioned.

Awards and Recognition. Successful student affairs offices rarely publish an issue of a newsletter or post staff meeting minutes in which there is not recognition of a faculty member who made a difference to students by introducing a new instructional technique, by working with student affairs to implement a program or service, or by volunteering to sponsor a campus club or organization. Whenever faculty members participate in or assist with a student affairs activity at most community colleges, they receive a certificate of appreciation from the chief student affairs officer (CSAO). More important, the CSAO writes a letter of appreciation to the faculty member's supervisor. One community college dean has printed cards with the message "Caught You" on the front and "Helping a Student Succeed" on the inside. The dean tries to catch faculty and staff members doing good things for and with students, then sends the card with a note outlining what she has seen. Another dean allocates space for a "Victory Wall" in the student services office and invites students to post thank you notes to faculty who help them achieve academic or personal victories.

Research the Positive. Instead of talking to students who withdraw to find out why they leave, some community colleges ask the students who remain in college what motivates them to stay. The data gathered is shared with faculty and staff members and becomes the catalyst for productive discussions about retention strategies. Looking at what actually works reduces the possibility that faculty will feel attacked and makes it more likely that they will be able to examine the data objectively.

THE PROMISES AND PITFALLS OF INFILTRATING
ACADEME AND BUILDING PARTNERSHIPS

Community college student affairs practitioners have discovered that partnerships between faculty and student affairs work when they are built on
mutual understanding and respect. Our college and university colleagues
need, however, to be aware that the very strategies that student affairs practitioners use to infiltrate academe can be turned against them in economically challenging times. For example: Student affairs staff members always make special efforts to establish partnerships and in doing so are
willing to assume the role of junior partners. This can create the impres-
sion that student affairs is inferior or subordinate to academic affairs.

Initially, student affairs staff members earn faculty respect by meeting or exceeding faculty expectations in the basic areas: admissions, advising, financial aid, orientation, and registration. For some, this establishes a
baseline beyond which student affairs should not go, particularly in eras
characterized by tight budgets.

Part of breaking down barriers involves training faculty to supplement the efforts of student affairs members during peak registration sea-
sons and to assume some of the responsibilities of the staff members in
their classrooms and offices. Some college presidents view the growing
sophistication of faculty in the student affairs arena as an opportunity to
slash the student affairs staff by transferring basic student affairs responsibilities to the faculty.

Community college student affairs staff members work at the leading edge of education. They are the first to identify new student trends,
community challenges, and campus problems. Often, their global perspective differs significantly from the view obtained from a faculty member's
classroom. When the partnership and the economy are strong, such differing views produce a creative tension that strengthens both student and academic affairs; when the partnership and the economy are weak, however,
the differing views produce clashes and dissension. An easy solution to
conflict involves the devaluation of the importance of the student affairs
function.

To maintain its identity and remain true to its mission as it infiltrates
and establishes partnerships with academe, a student affairs department
needs strong leadership. Too often, however, college presidents view the
desire of student affairs to collaborate with the faculty as an opportunity
for moving student affairs under academic affairs, eliminating the dean or
vice-president of student services, and replacing partnership with a subser-
vient role.

CONCLUSION

If the experiences of student affairs practitioners in community colleges demonstrate that partnerships between academic affairs and student affairs are a risk for student affairs, why would practitioners in colleges and universities even consider infiltrating academe? There are two answers to that question: first, although the risks are high, the potential rewards are higher and, second, it's the right thing to do. As this chapter has pointed out, students affairs practitioners and faculty members view the world through different, though complementary, lenses. Each has a piece of the teaching-learning-student success puzzle. Only when each learns to understand, respect, and value what the other has to offer will educational institutions become places where all students, not just those from privileged backgrounds, have the opportunity to succeed.

Because of their mission, student affairs staffs in community colleges had to meet the challenge of understanding and infiltrating academe long before their college and university colleagues began to discuss the relationship between student affairs and the teaching and learning process. College and university practitioners must move quickly to infiltrate academe, create partnerships, and develop programs to attract, retain, and graduate students who, a decade ago, would not have considered attending their colleges. The alternative is to face a slow death as institutions shift resources to support instruction.

References

Alfred, R. L., & Carter, P. (1997). Out of the box: Strategies for building high performing colleges. *Community College Journal, 67*(5), 41-47.

American College Personnel Association. (1994). *The student learning imperative: Implications for student affairs.* Washington, DC: Author.

Astin, A. W. (1993). *What matters in college: Four critical years revisited.* San Francisco: Jossey-Bass.

Blake, E. S. (1996, November-December). The yin and yang of student learning in college. *About Campus, 1,* 4-9.

Bloland, P. A., Stamatakos, L. C., & Rogers, R. R. (1994). *Reform in student affairs.* Greensboro, NC: ERIC Counseling and Student Services Clearinghouse.

Boggs, G. R. (1995). The learning paradigm. *Community College Journal, 66*(3), 24-27.

Culp, M. M,. & Helfgot, S. R. (1995). Focus on partnerships: looking in, looking out. In S. R. Helfgot and M. M. Culp (Eds.). *Promoting student success in the community college* (pp. 77-98). San Francisco: Jossey-Bass.

Ellis, D. B. (1985). *Becoming a master student*. Rapid City, SD: College Survival.

Hutchings, P. (1996, November-December). Building a new culture of teaching and learning. *About Campus, 1*, 4-8.

Kuh, G. D. (1996, September-October). Some things we should forget. *About Campus, 1*, 10-15.

Lorenzo, A. L., & LeCroy, N. A. (1994). A framework for fundamental change in the community college. *Community College Journal, 64*(4), 14-19.

O'Banion, T. (1994). Teaching and learning: A mandate for the nineties. *Community College Journal, 64*(4), 21-25.

Roueche, J. E., & Roueche, S. D. (1993). *Between a rock and a hard place*. Washington, DC: American Association of Community Colleges.

CHAPTER FIVE

Nests for Dreams, Backdrops for Visions

Making a Difference with Students

by Jack J. Becherer and Janna Hoekstra Becherer

How do community college student affairs programs make a difference? The answer lies in the way they serve complex students from diverse backgrounds. Consider these three representative student profiles.

Dashon and Jennifer are unmarried teenage students with a ten-month-old baby. Both attend college full time. Both have full-time jobs. Jennifer is Caucasian and works for a shipping organization from 9 p.m. to 5 a.m.; Dashon is African American and works for a grocery store from mid-afternoon into the evening. Each lives with his or her own parents and the baby lives with Dashon, whose mother provides primary care. Jennifer goes to Dashon's house daily after work and spends time with the baby before going to classes. Both arrive at their morning classes looking tired and disheveled.

Sara is taking nine semester hours at her community college. She is the single parent of a three-year-old son with asthma. Her son often needs to use his breathing machine three or four times a day, and the staff members at her current child care center are reluctant to provide this service because insurance regulations prohibit their engaging in an action that incurs a possible liability. Sara wonders if she will have to drop out of college to care for her son.

Erasmo owns a moderately successful motorcycle repair shop. When he turned 50, two years ago, he vowed to finally earn his college degree. During his first visit to a counselor at his local community college, he explained that his goal is to find work "that uses my brain more and my body less." Erasmo's college entrance tests led him straight into remedial courses in reading, English, and math. Undaunted, he completed those classes, making extensive use of the college's tutoring and returning adult services. Now he is enrolled full time in transferable courses and works out three times a week at the college fitness center while still running his business. "After all these years, a whole new world of learning is opening up to me," he recently told his counselor. "I feel like a kid in a candy store; I want to try it all."

Student affairs makes a difference by asking and answering a simple question: What do these students and others like them who enter our colleges need to help them succeed? The answer is found in a variety of services and programs that offer structure and support but this answer keeps growing more complex, partly because our students' lives are so complex, partly because the odds against their success are often so great, and partly because they seek convenient, cost-effective, and high quality education. In fact, in an interview, Ron Bleed referred to "swirling students" in the Phoenix metropolitan area who often bounce among the ten Maricopa Community Colleges and Arizona State University taking their courses based on "low cost, convenience and availability rather than the identity of the institution" (Rooney, 1996, p. 5).

Examples abound of innovative and exciting community college student affairs programs that make a difference, some by contributing to student learning, others by helping students to overcome barriers, and still others by simplifying student transitions to another college or to the world of work. Many of these programs parallel those offered at four-year colleges and universities. Some difference-making programs, however, such as those designed to assist returning adults, under-represented populations, or students with multiple priorities, may not often be found at residential colleges and therefore provide a potential learning opportunity for those enrolled at such institutions.

As diverse as these effective student affairs initiatives may be, three categories of programs stand out as best demonstrating the differences between those typically offered at community colleges and those traditionally available at four-year colleges:

- Programs providing unique holding environments that embrace students and nurture their success.

- Programs addressing the challenges that accompany the implied promise of an open-door philosophy.
- Programs establishing vibrant partnerships with local communities.

PROVIDING A HOLDING ENVIRONMENT

Meeting the needs of students at community colleges requires a ready-response mentality and a willingness to treat students as highly valued customers while at the same time providing a nurturing and flexible "holding environment" that fosters student development. Kegan (1982) describes a holding environment as any situation "where holding refers not to keeping or confining but to supporting (even 'floating' as in amniotic fluid) the exercises of who a person is" (p. 162). Programs and services that are intentionally designed to minimize student frustration, to foster student learning, and to maximize student success offer holding environments that serve our students well. Today's community colleges are actively re-engineering student affairs programs and services that create a climate for exercising learning and growth, sometimes without the student's awareness.

What does this look like in actual practice? Services are streamlined and designed for the students' lifestyles rather than for the traditional 8:00 a.m.-5:00 p.m. work schedule often favored by college employees; admission forms can be completed in five minutes rather than in two hours and can be entered into the college's student data system while the student waits; touch tone or web-based registration (such as that used at Moraine Valley Community College) is available so that students can register from home or between classes without waiting in long lines; new student orientation programs (like that used at Fullerton College) are offered where new students can choose among traditional orientation sessions with a counselor, a touch-screen orientation, available day and night, that uses a mastery learning approach, or a small group orientation format presented in students' native languages including Spanish and Vietnamese; free tutoring and academic assistance centers are staffed from 8:00 a.m. until 8:00 p.m. (South Suburban College); and the college child care center stays open until evening classes let out.

Well-designed holding environments also promote student success when they target particular subgroups of students who are clearly at risk of stopping or dropping out before reaching their academic goals. Community colleges across America offer such environments in abundance. They include the new Buckner Family Place that assists families — especially "those headed by single women" — to step out of domestically violent environments and into a calmer, safer place that offers food, housing, child care, and counseling (Cvancara, 1997, p. 14). Students attending Angelina College in rural East Texas can stay at Buckner Place while pursuing their degrees. In an article that describes the collaborative efforts to found Buckner Place, Angelina's president, Larry Phillips, notes that "about 10 percent of the college's students are in need of basic necessities, such as housing and food. Those students can't concentrate on their homework at the same time they're worried over finding their next meal" (Cvancara, 1997, p. 14). The Buckner Family Place initiative goes the extra mile so students can move closer to their educational and career goals, eventually becoming capable of earning a regular income and creating a stable home life.

Another highly functional holding environment operates at the College of San Mateo, where the Transition to College program boasts an 83 percent retention rate for students who have had their education interrupted by mental illnesses such as schizophrenia and manic depression. In this unusual, focused program, a combination of supplemental classes, peer support, and educational accommodations has helped many students with psychological disabilities to meet their career and personal goals. According to Tim Stringari, coordinator of San Mateo's Psychological Services office, this is a remarkable achievement for students whose attrition rate has traditionally been "exceptionally high as a result of anxiety, low stress tolerance, lack of academic and social skills, and low self-esteem" (Stringari, 1997, p. 1). At least 75 percent of the students in the Transition to College program had been unsuccessful in previous attempts at completing before enrolling in San Mateo's program. Since the program began in 1991, over 600 students have benefited from the special class sections on college orientation and study skills, disability management, and peer-led support groups. Students report that the encouragement and support they received were most helpful in developing their self-confidence in the college environment and in making the transition into regular college classes.

Still another beneficial holding environment derives from the joint effort to address the problems raised by welfare reform by Monroe Community College and the local Department of Social Services. The college's Temporary Assistance for Student Careers (TASC) program helps move public assistance recipients to work through community college degree, certificate, and short-term training programs. This program involves collaboration between the student services department, which administers an on-campus work experience component, and examiners from the Department of Social Service, who conduct assessments in offices at Monroe. Ongoing support, follow-up, and counseling are provided to students by

both groups, evidence of a holding environment that simplifies government requirements and allows students to make progress.

THE CHALLENGE OF OPEN ACCESS

Community colleges typically espouse a philosophy of allowing open access to all those who can benefit from their programs. As a result, students
enter these institutions with a broad array of skills, abilities, and experiences, with many requiring preparatory work in reading, writing, or mathematics before attempting college-level courses. According to an October
1996 report by the National Center for Education Statistics, 41 percent
(386,000 students) of first-time community college freshmen enroll in some
kind of preparatory course (Lazarick, 1997). At some community colleges,
remedial courses represent a majority of all courses offered (Whitman,
1989).

This policy contrasts with that of four-year colleges and universities,
which traditionally use admissions standards to select students who appear
to be ready to meet the demands of their curriculum. The assumptions
behind these two admissions philosophies are quite different, as are the
responsibilities that follow from these assumptions.

Because they may assume that students possess the skills and resources
to successfully complete their courses, colleges with selective admissions
policies do not need to develop extensive programs designed to prepare
students to achieve success. Community colleges, on the other hand, must
develop comprehensive preparatory programs given that they may know-
ingly admit students who do not possess the skills to succeed at college-
level coursework.

Over 20 years ago, Ed Glazer, then president of the American Association of Community Colleges, defined the most critical challenge of the
community college as making good on the implied promise of the open
door (Rouesche & Rouesche, 1993, p. 18). The challenge today is no less
critical; changing demographics and a faltering public education system
have resulted in an even broader mix of students and higher percentages of
matriculated students who require college preparatory coursework. Roueche
and Roueche (1993) conclude that these issues pose a dilemma for the
institutions, with access being more critical than in the past and the responsibilities of open admission more overwhelming.

Not all community colleges respond in the same way to these pressures. Mandatory assessment in reading, writing, and mathematics is common among community colleges, with mandatory placement in remedial

programs, when indicated, more the norm than the exception. Few colleges, however, go beyond identifying the academic deficiencies to address other issues that clearly affect academic performance. These issues are far-ranging and complex, including students' lack of confidence, unfocused goals, difficulty adjusting to school, financial complications, and feelings of isolation, along with students having not yet mastered the techniques of learning.

Extraordinary community college student affairs programs have accepted the challenge of addressing these barriers to success. For example, Holyoke Community College responded to student needs that go beyond academics by expanding their assessment program, not only testing for basic skills but also for other factors that influence student success. New students at Holyoke complete a Student Needs Inventory (SNI) designed to assess needs and interests in 25 different areas where the college can provide services, in addition to a computerized assessment in basic skills. Also, demographic data and requests for additional information are gathered in the SNI.

Assessment data is electronically collated and used for multiple purposes, all designed to promote the students' level of involvement in the college's programs and in their own quest for success. Initially, the basic skill and demographic data are combined to identify high-risk students. Prior to the beginning of classes, students meet with an educational planner who advises them on academic programs, schedules their classes, and discusses possible referrals to various college services. Since the SNI becomes part of the student's educational plan, the faculty has access to this information in later advising sessions.

Particularly important is the use of the assessment data after the student begins classes. At Holyoke, student affairs staff members do not wait for students to solicit their services. They receive weekly listings, with mailing labels, of all students whose profiles indicate that a service might be helpful. These listings enable staff members to reach out to such students personally. Outreach efforts continue throughout the first semester, keeping students informed of opportunities for assistance while assuring them that a nurturing support structure is available when needed.

Holyoke's combination of student needs and basic skills assessment, followed by supportive outreach and referral efforts, provides an excellent example of how to make good on the implied promises of the open door. Furthermore, its creative use of technology facilitates the establishment of a needs profile for the entire student body. Thus, assessment results provide a powerful planning tool, transcending individual needs, to establish priorities for the use of student development resources.

Baltimore City Community College's student affairs division addresses the challenge of access by offering specially designed support groups for new students. The groups, called Women of Strength and Positive Men, incorporate collaborative learning techniques, development of higher-order thinking, and peer tutoring to foster goal attainment and academic achievement. Groups meet weekly and exchange views on pre-arranged topics, including parenting, attitudinal healing, medical/health challenges, and academic excellence. Service learning experiences and other community involvement initiatives are integrated into the group experience.

Students are provided with the tools and strategies they need to make positive and lasting changes in themselves, as a supplement to their academic experiences. Participants typically perceive barriers to their success, and whether these are real or merely psychological they must be overcome. Networking skills and problem-solving skills that can be applied during their college careers and after are developed. Alicia Harvey-Smith, one of the program's creators, describes the Women of Strength and the Positive Men groups as "nests for dreams, backdrops for visions, launching pads for ambitions and platforms for creative expression, providing an opportunity to talk, laugh, listen, rejoice, commiserate and celebrate with the experience of womanhood or manhood" (Harvey-Smith, 1997, p. 2).

This group experience works, as is demonstrated by a retention rate of 85 percent from one academic year to the next. Students report an improved ability to organize, promote the fulfillment of their own personal needs, achieve academically, and establish a proactive approach to life. Clearly, Baltimore City Community College goes beyond providing basic services in its efforts to help students who walk through its open door to achieve success.

Lansing Community College's Women's Resource Center provides yet another example of reaching beyond what is normally expected in its attempts to promote student success. The Women's Resource Center, located at an off-campus urban downtown location, for the most part serves women who are low income, between the ages of 25 and 44, and single, divorced, widowed, or separated. Most have had some, often unsuccessful, college experience, and at least 70 percent are identified as academically disadvantaged and as requiring coursework in developmental reading, writing, or both.

The Women's Resource Center is a re-entry center with a mission summarized by the motto, "If everyone deserves another chance, let's give them a good one!" Basic skills and career assessment initially provides a realistic picture of the students' potential and the challenges that must be met to reach that potential. Financial assistance is then sought to address such critical needs as child care, textbooks, tuition, or transportation. The center's success in identifying sources of aid is especially noteworthy, since many of its students are ineligible for federal grants and loans due to the lack of success in earlier educational endeavors. Once financial resources are established, the five professional staff members of the center employ a case management approach to effectively address each student's needs. Although a student is not assigned to a specific staff member, every contact is carefully documented, providing a detailed history which any staff member can call upon to further develop the relationship between the student and the center.

Services extend beyond comprehensive assessment, financial support, and personalized case management. Back-to-school workshops orient students to the challenges involved in returning to school. Friendships and self-esteem develop through support groups. Workshops are offered that address topics of domestic violence, parenting, health concerns, legal issues regarding divorce, and employment skills. Mandatory advising ensures careful course selection based on individual needs, goals, and circumstances. Progress reports from faculty suggest the need for tutoring, counseling, or emergency family intervention.

Lansing's Women's Resource Center clearly makes a full effort to assist students who re-enter college through its open door. The comprehensive array of services offered creates a nurturing environment that provides re-entering students with a legitimate second chance. Data collected annually indicates that 80 percent of the program participants meet Lansing's academic standards, providing strong evidence of the positive impact that a thoughtfully designed, highly structured, and skillfully implemented student affairs program can have.

STAYING CLOSE TO THE COMMUNITY

In a recent article, Rifkin (1996) praises the way community colleges nourish their connections with local residents, schools, and civic organizations.

> Community colleges will likely play a critical role in reshaping American education and laying the groundwork for the renewal of a civil society. Unlike many four-year colleges, where the relationship between town and gown is often distant and strained, community colleges, for the most part, are deeply involved in the civic life of the community (p. 22).

O'Banion and Gillett-Karam (1986) have examined the role and effectiveness of community colleges' service to their communities, including cases of community college efforts to establish a community presence for addressing social issues such as racial conflict, inadequate housing, addictive behaviors, and poverty. In addition, they cite community colleges that bring to their communities economic development activities that transcend the emphasis on educational services of the traditional institutional model. These authors are not convinced, however, that the majority of community colleges do much more than offer credit and non-credit courses that meet the postsecondary educational needs of the diverse communities they serve. They write that "most community colleges today still do not play key roles as community agencies of social change in areas of complex social issues except to provide traditional educational services such as courses, forums and publications to address these issues" (p. 34). O'Banion and Gillett-Karam clearly urge institutions to seize opportunities for extended involvement with the cities, towns, and villages in which they are located.

Such deep involvement is evident in the San Jacinto College District through an annual "Project Start Trek" held for area eighth graders. Using creative and entertaining 20-minute programs, the college introduces nearly 6,000 eighth graders to various career opportunities, encourages them to pursue higher education, reinforces the value of the math, reading, and writing skills, and encourages the students to begin thinking about their life goals. According to Brooke Zemel, the director of counseling, testing, and placement at San Jacinto, sessions include "Education Pays," in which participants compare the income levels, taxes, and purchasing power typical of high school dropouts to those who have earned associates, bachelors, masters, and professional degrees. Other programs feature an Elvis Presley impersonator, who emphasizes communication skills, and a Darth Vader character, played by a member of the college's math faculty, who promotes the importance of science and math in everyday life using compact disc players, computers, and big screen televisions. These sessions build bridges between young students, parents, schools, and the community college.

Bridges are also built when colleges incorporate service learning into various student development and academic programs. Lane Community College in Oregon accomplishes this in its African American Rites of Passage Summer Academy for ninth- and tenth-graders. The academy, a joint project between Lane and the local African American Community Coalition, offers participants classes in "math, writing, public speaking, African-American history . . . spirituality, cross-cultural communications, violence, AIDS and other topics" (Evans, 1997). These courses are taught by faculty from Lane and Oregon State University, and by members of the community. The service learning component includes removing graffiti from downtown buildings, a real life exercise in restoring the urban environment, and it represents a successful partnership among the college, the university, and the community.

Another urban environment was much improved when the Albuquerque Technical-Vocational Institute (T-VI) spearheaded an initiative with the city and local neighborhood associations (Tangman, 1993). Initially, local residents were mistrustful of T-VI's overtures, fearing that the college's expansion plans would ignore the needs of the surrounding neighborhoods. Wary residents were first surprised, and finally, after a year of negotiation, won over by T-VI's persistent efforts to seek mutually beneficial solutions. After countless meetings and a range of proposals generated by both sides, an agreement was reached to refurbish a decrepit community center and a litter-strewn dirt lot adjacent to T-VI. The local community gained a vibrant facility where residents take exercise classes, enjoy social events, upgrade skills, and watch their children play on new outdoor playground equipment, while the college gained much-needed classroom space in the community center building. The college has also built a separate child care center on the property that serves both low-income T-VI students and local families. Clearly, in this partnership, both "town" and "gown" come out winners.

In the San Antonio area, women living in the public housing projects are now able to take selected community college courses at the projects thanks to San Antonio College's Second Chance program. The Second Chance staff, including a program counselor, part-time mentor/tutor, and two part-time clerks, works closely with the San Antonio Housing Authority Family and Self-Sufficiency Program, which recruits the students and provides the classroom facilities. This collaboration enables students to take courses in a familiar environment, avoiding the transportation and child care problems that often cause new students to give up their college careers. Among the characteristic features of the program are mandatory weekly self-assessment and tutoring sessions that help fledgling students cope with family and academic concerns. According to Olga Flores Garcia, who initiated the Second Chance program, these students "need somebody to hold their hand, at least for the first semester" (Schmidt, 1996, p. A8).

Community connections can also include partnerships with high schools and universities. For example, Northwest Arkansas Community College has established a Step Ahead partnership program with area secondary schools. This seamless transfer program gives high school students the option to begin their college studies on their high school campuses by taking college core courses whose credits can be transferred. High school juniors and seniors with at least a "B" average and the recommendation of their counselor or principal can enroll in up to seven college credit hours per semester. Since the college has developed a dual enrollment plan with the University of Arkansas, participants know they are accumulating credits that can be transferred to either their local community college or to a premier state university.

As two-year colleges continue their deep involvement with surrounding communities, everyone benefits. Learning opportunities are broadened and enhanced, chances for student success are increased, and the civic life of the community is enriched.

RESEARCH
The Missing Element in Community College Student Affairs

Although it is evident that student affairs programs make a difference, few community colleges determine the extent of this difference and fewer still know the key variables that lead to their success. Thus, student affairs administrators who develop and implement extraordinary programs take note of the resulting positive outcomes, such as high levels of satisfaction, satisfactory academic progress, or continued enrollment, but they usually do not attempt to explain what aspects of the program are responsible for these outcomes. Student affairs programs are not unique in this regard. Spence and Campbell (1996) note that "American colleges and universities hold one central goal in common . . . to help students learn. Rarely, however, do institutions attempt to discover whether or how much their students are learning" (p. 26).

Most of the student affairs programs described in this chapter document the outcomes for their participants; for example, Lansing Community College's Women Resource Center has determined that 80 percent of its program participants meet academic standards, and the College of San Mateo's Transition to College Program boasts an 83 percent retention rate for students with mental illness. Data collected regarding student success, however, critical though it is, does little to explain the causal factors behind the positive outcomes. Thus, student affairs practitioners often know that their work has benefitted students but have little information about exactly which program components led to those benefits.

Some community colleges are attempting to go beyond identifying outcomes by establishing benchmarks that, if achieved, would indicate programmatic success. For example, Santa Fe New Mexico Community College uses a program development model to study the anticipated impact of new programs, services, and events. This model tests new enterprises for relevance to the teaching-learning mission of the college and for congruence with the service-oriented principles within the student services department. In addition, any proposed program must demonstrate responsiveness to the characteristics of adult learners and to the increasing diversity of the students the school serves. Establishing standards of relevance and expectations for learning allows the student services team to develop programs with specific anticipated outcomes in a highly focused manner. Assessment of these programs not only documents what has been achieved in terms of mastery of learning objectives, improved in-term retention, or sustained persistence but also compares what has been achieved to what was anticipated, providing a new control on program effectiveness.

Seidman (1993) asserts that research questions should be clearly defined prior to collecting outcome data. "In an era of diminishing resources and a growing urgency to improve the quality of post-secondary education, it is important to use criteria that best judge institutional effectiveness" (p. 39). Furthermore, this author suggests that collecting pre-entry academic, personal goal, and skill data can help determine the impact of a service on students with diverse intents and varying abilities. Over time, wise use of this data would lead to the development of specific programs to assist students with a particular profile of goals and skills. Grouping students in this manner and designing programs specifically based on particular profiles holds great promise for enhanced program effectiveness and greater student achievement and success.

Roueche and Roueche (1993) view program evaluation as a thorny issue that deserves more attention than it receives, stating that "even more unfortunate than the curious infrequency with which successful, time-honored teaching and learning strategies are implemented is the continuing inattention to careful evaluation of our services to all students" and concluding that "as painful as the process — and the resulting discoveries — may be, thoughtful evaluation is the only reasonable plan by which inappropriate directions, decisions or activities be corrected" (pp. 21-22).

Assessment does not have to be a painful process. Student affairs practitioners can go beyond knowing that their programs are useful to knowing what specific aspects make a difference — and with which students. They can develop research designs to investigate why an intervention contributed to changes in student attitudes, beliefs, and actions, ask thoughtful questions that lead to focused data collection, and, finally, use assessment of existing programs and services to chart future directions.

CONCLUSION

As the preceding examples show, extraordinary student affairs departments in community colleges create exemplary programs to assist students in unique and distinctive ways. Programs that provide nurturing, attentive, and caring holding environments support students as they develop the attitudes, behaviors, and self-esteem necessary for success in college. In addition, these programs make good on the promise of the open door and offer much more than remedial and developmental instruction to ensure students' success in transferring to a four-year institution or fulfilling their occupational goals. Finally, departments that make a difference join with community and civic organizations, elementary and secondary educational systems, other colleges and universities, and churches and advocacy groups to resolve the complex and challenging problems that can threaten the fabric of a community or restrict the quality of its citizens' lives.

Too few student affairs programs at any level go beyond ordinary efforts to promote student success through creative efforts such as those highlighted in this chapter. Student affairs practitioners in four-year colleges, like their colleagues from community colleges, can learn new approaches from these extraordinary community college student affairs programs. The authors have identified six key characteristics that distinguish extraordinary from average student affairs programs. Those programs that excel involve: a) champions who lead the way; b) creative, nontraditional programs that meet student needs; c) intentional learning environments that foster student action; d) inclusiveness and the elicitation of a sense of belonging that promotes student success; e) collaborations that increase options for students, faculty and staff members; and, f) a clear, focused mission that provides a sense of direction (Becherer & Becherer, 1995, p. 64). These key characteristics can be used to instill new life into existing programs or as guidelines when developing new programs and services.

Both community college and four-year college student affairs administrators should consider ways to learn more about the good work at their colleges. Too little time is devoted to learning from each other. Undoubtedly, there are more similarities than differences in the work that we do and, for a start, we could learn a great deal by attending each other's programs at professional conferences. Also, we could make use of each other's publications when doing research. Finally, we could share the mission and perspectives of our institutions with the student affairs practitioners in-training at our graduate schools.

It would be a mistake to consider the work of student affairs professionals at community and four-year colleges as a we/they issue. We are united in our goal to promote student success. By identifying and emulating exceptional programs, especially leading edge programs in community colleges, promoting the impact of our discipline on student success, and celebrating our common activities, the student affairs function will remain vital to all postsecondary institutions.

References

Becherer, J. & Becherer, J.H. (1995). Programs, services and activities: A survey of the community college landscape. In S. R. Helfgot & M. M. Culp (Eds.). *Promoting student success in the community college. (*New Directions in Student Services, no. 69) (pp. 63-75). San Francisco: Jossey-Bass.

Cvancara, K. (1997). Looking for guidance on their own. *Community College Journal, 67*(4), 8-14.

Evans, G. (1997, Summer). Community outreach: A summer academy at Lane Community College. *Linkages, 20,* 1.

Harvey-Smith, A. (1997). Women of strength and positive men: Reinforcing the open access mission with a tailored approach. Unpublished Manuscript, Baltimore City Community College, Baltimore MD.

Kegan, R. (1982). *The Evolving Self.* Cambridge, MA: Harvard University Press.

Lazarick, L. (1997). Back to the basics: Remedial education. *Community College Journal, 68*(2), 11-15.

O'Banion, T., & Gillett-Karam, R. (1986). The people's college and the street people: Community colleges and community development. *Community College Journal, 67*(2), 33-37.

Rifkin, J. (1996). Preparing the next generation of students for the civil society. *Community College Journal, 66*(5), 20-22.

Rooney, M. (1996). Technology pushes new roles for student services professionals: An interview with Ron Bleed. *Eleven Update, 7*(2), 3-5.

Roueche, J., & Roueche, S. (1993). Making good on the promise: The view between a rock and a hard place. *Community College Journal, 63*(5), 18-23.

Schmidt, P. (October 4, 1996). Reaching students in public housing. *The Chronicle of Higher Education, 43,* A8.

Seidman, A. (1993). A research methodology to assess community college effectiveness. *Community College Journal, 63*(5), 36-40.

Spence, C., & Campbell, D. (1996). Building learning communities: Indicators for a new vision for community colleges. *Community College Journal, 67*(2), 24-27.

Stringari, T. (1997). Mental illness: No longer a barrier to a college education. Unpublished Manuscript, The College of San Mateo, San Mateo, CA.

Tangman, R. (1993). Beyond building communities. *Community College Journal, 64*(3), 12-16.

Whitman, D. (June 26, 1989). The forgotten half. *U. S. News and World Report,* 45.

CHAPTER SIX

———◆———

Tools for Tomorrow
Re-envisioning the Student Body

by Steven R. Helfgot

Throughout this volume, the authors have repeatedly referred to the new students who populate community college campuses and who are, increasingly, enrolling in colleges and universities as well. It is one thing to understand that a particular student may be a recent immigrant/first-time college-goer, a welfare recipient on a fast-track program for career training, or a single mother going to school while working full time and caring for her family. It is quite another thing to envision the entire student body, or at least large portions of the student body, in terms like these; and it is still another thing to move from that understanding to conceptualizing the delivery of programs and services to such a heterogeneous and diverse set of students. In this final chapter, we will look at a set of professional "tools for tomorrow" and will begin with some words of caution and suggestions about how student affairs practitioners need to view and conceptualize the students who, with growing frequency, are becoming the wave of students in all institutions of higher learning.

THE TRADITIONAL VIEW
The Student Body

For years, particularly in colleges and universities, each institution had a student body with a particular profile. Of course, students generally were between the ages of 18 and 22 and of a certain ability level. Some colleges admitted only those with the very best grades and test scores, while others offered admission to students scoring in lower percentiles or quartiles, based on different combinations of grades and scores. Financial aid made it possible for students from different socioeconomic groups to enter, and special programs were established to provide support for specific groups of students. The working assumption seemed to be that students would adjust to the institution's culture; that the opposite should happen — that the institution should somehow adjust to or make accommodations for differing students — seemed not to be considered. The students, after all, were not really that different from one another: some might go "Greek" and others "independent," some live on campus and others in off-campus apartments but, taken together, regardless of their numbers, they were "the student body."

We in student affairs, although taught to appreciate, value, and work with individual differences, often succumbed to this belief. We programmed for the student body, tried to determine the needs of the student body, and considered what might be most effective with our particular student body. The temptation, therefore, was always to equate success with size. If a dance or a concert was well attended, it was a success. If a large number of students participated in new student orientation, a faculty advising program, or a career planning seminar, then we had succeeded. If some students did not participate, the assumption was that they were uninterested or unmotivated or somehow uninvolved. The program, activity, or service, however, was the right one because it so clearly appealed to so many members of the student body. With the rapid growth of community colleges and their waves of new, nontraditional students that view has changed radically and possibly forever.

DIVERSE STUDENTS, DIVERSE GROUPS, DIVERSE NEEDS
Re-envisioning the Student Body

As community colleges began to appear in nearly every community in the 1960s and 1970s, the very definition of what it meant to be a college student changed: attending college no longer required leaving home or engaging in a lengthy commute. Those who thought that the opportunity to go to college had passed them by — adults with families and careers — could now reasonably expect to begin a college career without having to sacrifice their lives and lifestyles.

Those who thought that college was not for them because they did not have the preparation, the grades, or the money, now saw a door to higher education open to them. The community colleges were different, as were their students, who were sometimes different from the traditional notion of what a college student was and always very different from one another. Sometimes, indeed much of the time, it was impossible to predict what type of students they were.

At Cerritos College, California, where I have worked for the past 12 years, some of the students I have known are these:

A 68-year old grandmother was our homecoming queen. Having grown up during the depression, she had never had the opportunity to go to college. After raising a family and retiring from the business that she and her husband had run for years, she decided to go to college — and she jumped in with both feet, not just going to class but joining student clubs and writing for the student newspaper. Enthusiastic, articulate, and charming, she became a well-known figure on campus. She was nominated for homecoming queen and elected by her fellow students, not as a joke but because she was such a wonderful representative.

In 1996-97, the student government president/student trustee was a retired Marine Corps captain in his mid-40s. His story is much the same as that of the homecoming queen grandmother, that of a nontraditional student who wanted to have the traditional college experience that had been unavailable to him earlier. He, too, was active in several areas, most notably as a prize-winning member of the college's speech and debate team.

A National Honor Society student came to our college directly from high school in the 1970s, even though she could have gone to any number of universities with a substantial scholarship. I met her some ten years later as she was finishing her requirements for both an AA degree and for transfer to the university. She had completed these requirements taking one course per semester, every semester for ten years, and she had received an "A" in every course. All the while she had continued to work for the telephone company as an operator, the job she had held since she graduated from high school. She came to campus, went to class, and went home or back to work. She never joined a club, never attended a football game, never went to a lecture. She had been able to come to college as an 18-year old living at home only if she had a good job that she could "fall back on" and that could help her pay for her education. Why? As she explained it, in her family a college education was seen as frivolous for a girl. Even as an adult approaching 30, she had continued to pursue her education in accordance with the rules established when she was 18. Now faced with the possibility of going on to the university to finish her education — and perhaps look at a new career — she was struggling with the possibility of breaking the rules, quitting work, living on her savings, and going to school full time.

Finally, one young man who was enrolled in our Automotive Technology program would, semester after semester (as I later learned), show up in the class of one of our philosophy professors and ask to sit in on the class. Somehow he prevailed on the professor who, having found out that I was this student's counselor, came to speak with me about him. This student, while not even enrolled in the professor's class, was, for all intents and purposes, his best student, indeed, one of his best ever. When next I saw the student, I asked about this strange situation. It turned out that he was a gang member who had been given the opportunity by a judge to learn a trade rather than go to jail. So, while he took his "Auto Tech" classes, he discovered accidentally that he had a passion for philosophy. He was afraid to actually enroll in the courses because he was worried that this would be seen as breaking the deal he had with the judge.

There is nothing extraordinary about these examples; there is not a community college student affairs administrator who could not share similarly incongruous stories about students they have known. As is clear from all of these cases, the diversification of student bodies at all institutions requires that we see students in new ways. Following are a few suggestions about how to re-envision students and student bodies:

• *Think small when thinking about students.* The more diverse the students are, the smaller the group with which a particular student identifies. That is, there may not be a single student body on a given campus, but ten, twenty, or fifty, depending on the criterion or definition being used. Thus, a program or service that effectively serves fifty, a hundred, or even twenty students effectively may be a huge success.

• *Think big (or, at least, multiple) when thinking about programs and services.* One size does not fit all. For example, a new student orientation may be a good idea for every new student but, as suggested elsewhere in this monograph, it may need to be available in multiple forms and formats: both a long form and a short one may be necessary; it may have to be offered days and evenings and weekends; it may require providing it on a CD, on-line, on cable television, and on videocassette; and it may have to be available in any number of languages.

• *Things are not always what they seem.* There will be 45 year old students who want to be student government leaders and 18 year olds who want a no-frills education, little involvement on campus, and consumer oriented service on-demand.

• *Etch nothing in stone; write only in pencil and do not become overly invested in last year's great idea.* Do not assume that a program, a service, a particular approach will work for five years, two years, or even two semesters. Change is the only constant. Last year's wonderfully successful approach may fall flat this year. Its success is not diminished by that fact; it may simply be that students have changed again.

• *Scan the environment over and over and over.* To start, read the demographics on your students. It helps to know if the percentage of adult students or minority students is rising, for example, but that information, by itself, is inconclusive. Wander around; talk to students, to professors, and to other staff members. What do the outreach and recruitment staff have to say about each particular group? Use surveys and focus groups and interviews to find out what these students need and want this semester. Then do it again next semester, and the semester after that, and so on.

• *Be willing to go where no one has gone before.* What may seem like a strange new world out there may, indeed, be a strange new world. New students in new combinations with new needs may lead to programs and to ways of delivering services that are without precedent (at least on a particular campus). Resist the temptation of the low risk, of the tried and true. They may not be worth the effort. For example, although leadership retreats may be commonplace, leadership retreats that involve family programming may be unheard of. If students in the leadership group are adults with families, however, a retreat that does not provide for family involvement may never happen. Just because it has not been done before does not mean it should not be done this time.

CONCLUSION

It might seem almost ludicrous to consider thinking as the first and most essential "tool for tomorrow" in student affairs work. But it is just that. Thinking in new ways about new students, programs, and services and in new ways about old programs and practices may well be the core skill for successful student affairs practice in the next century. With new thinking comes the possibility of new vision, and the ability to continuously re-envision a rapidly changing and dynamic student population.

PREPARING FUTURE COMMUNITY
COLLEGE PROFESSIONALS

by Cynthia S. Johnson

*I*n June 1997, the Senior Scholars of the American College Personnel Association (ACPA), with funding from the Fetzer Foundation, convened a Trends Analysis meeting whose participants included representatives from the American Association of Community Colleges (AACC), the National Association of Student Personnel Administrators (NASPA), the American Association of Higher Education (AAHE), the American Council on Education (ACE), and the Association of Governing Boards (AGB). At the meeting, participants concluded that community colleges were already addressing many of the trends that were beginning to have an impact on four-year colleges at present and that continue to remain issues for the institutions into the next century.

Of the eight identified trends, the two involving the achievement of widest possible access for students and affordability of education are already important to community colleges, with their diverse demographic profiles, their increasing numbers of immigrant students, and the awareness that they must serve a new wave of welfare recipients. Two additional trends, the need both for partnerships, exemplified in the kindergarten through 14th grade alliance of the Dallas Community College District, and the need for greater emphasis on teaching and learning, have long been at the top of two-year colleges' agendas.

Given these trends and similar ones, we need to explore how graduate school faculty members who are training a new generation of student affairs practitioners can learn from the ways their community college colleagues are already addressing the challenges presented by these trends, and how masters and doctoral programs can recruit and prepare practitioners who have the knowledge and skills that will be needed in the future in both two- and four-year institutions.

INCREASING NEED

A community college president recently stated that he was going to lose more than 20 percent of his faculty and staff members in the next five years because so many had been hired in the 1960s and were now approaching retirement. When asked where he was going to find new faculty, and what characteristics he wanted them to have, he replied, "Oh that won't be a problem. Many people will apply for those positions, and I will probably ask those who are leaving to help break in the new people." This is certainly not a visionary response, but it is perhaps understandable given the paucity of graduate training programs which focus on preparing practitioners for community colleges.

The need for a new generation of professionals in community colleges is well documented. Large numbers of new students, labeled Tidal Wave II, are expected on college campuses within the next ten years. In California alone, an additional 488,000 students are projected (California Higher Education Policy Center, 1996), many of whom will begin their postsecondary education in a community college. Moreover, the 1996 California Community College chancellor's office report indicated that 32-38 percent of the 43,000 faculty and staff members in the state will have retired by the beginning of the century.

Community colleges need a vision and included in that vision must be plans for the succession of a new generation of faculty and staff members. If, as many leaders have claimed, the emerging situation will not allow the conduct of business as usual, it will become necessary to gain a picture of what the new faculty and staff members will be like and what kind of knowledge and skills they will bring.

This monograph is not alone in its assertion that community colleges already have gained some of the expertise that will be needed to teach and serve the next wave of college students. The knowledge that has already been gained should be shared systematically with those whose role it is to prepare the faculty and staffs of the future, to help them understand that the knowledge, skills, and techniques currently in use in community colleges will soon also be needed in senior institutions.

THE ROLE OF GRADUATE PREPARATION PROGRAMS

Master's and doctoral programs can play at least three significant roles that will have a positive impact on the next generation of community college leaders:
- the redesign of current graduate programs and the development of new ones;
- the recruitment of students for graduate programs; and
- the involvement of graduate programs in professional and continuing education.

Redesigning Current Graduate Programs and Developing New Ones

Both new and existing programs must be encouraged to include courses on community colleges and their unique needs, developed in collaboration with those working in two-year institutions, and to include in their master's and doctoral curricula the information and skills that will prepare their students for the changing environment of higher education during the next century.

When asked in recent interviews what future faculty and staff members will need, community college leaders offered some of the following suggestions:

• They will have to place more emphasis on adult students and develop sensitivity to the multiple pressures and roles they juggle and the many sacrifices they undergo.

• They must have strong knowledge of technology and its role in student learning and use it to serve a diverse student population whose members have diverse needs.

• They will require up-to-date information about the latest wave of students: who they are (i.e., their diverse cultural heritages) how they learn (i.e., "ways of knowing"). The new students will include the immigrants who are now enrolling in large numbers in such places as the Miami-Dade County and Los Angeles City and other community college districts, as well as the welfare recipients who are beginning to enroll in large numbers in community colleges across the country.

• Student affairs staff members, counselors, and faculty members need to understand curriculum development, instructional design, and the use of self-paced learning modules. They must learn how to manage multiple roles and how to design individual plans for students who have very varied needs.

• They must place more emphasis on management skills, including time management, case load management, the encouragement of team work, collaboration, and partnership, and the institution of accountability measures.

• The new hires must understand the interconnectedness between the community served and its K-12 systems, its effect on today's community college students, and how to work with students who are concurrently enrolled in more than one institution.

• Current graduate students should be better trained to face the demands of the workplace of the future and to adjust to students from cultures that emphasize interdependent rather independent career decision making.

Also recommended was that new hires learn to be comfortable with change and complexity; commit themselves to being lifelong learners; know how to "work out of the box"; no longer seek refuge in their discipline; avoid being "solo players"; and have skills in outcomes assessment.

In a recent field work seminar, Than, a graduate student, said of her assignment on a community college campus: "My students range from 16 to 66 years of age; 20 percent can't read and yet a large number have undergraduate or graduate degrees, and some bring [to the classroom] psychological problems." Than and her future colleagues will have makes changes in course content and rethink the curriculum in order to help such students succeed. Moreover, given that a significant number of these students will transfer to a university, those planning to work in four-year schools will need similar preparation.

A more systematic attempt must be made to identify the skills and knowledge needed for the future without sacrificing the profession's existing histories, philosophies, and theories. While there are excellent graduate programs that focus on community colleges, more of them must place a greater emphasis on this important segment of higher education, especially given that the student population of many colleges and universities will increasingly resemble that population currently found in the community college.

GRADUATE SCHOOL RECRUITMENT

The second role for graduate programs involves making the effort to recruit students who share demographic traits with the community college students they are to serve, a requirement currently mandated by at least one state. While student affairs professional associations have developed written material and instituted career fairs as a means of recruiting students from population groups under-represented in the field, current graduate students are still not representative of the richly diverse student populations of current and future campuses. Many first-generation students are not aware of the career possibilities available in student affairs, although they may have themselves been inspired to complete their undergraduate education by a community college counselor or other staff member. Graduate faculty members must become more sophisticated about attracting and retaining students of color, older adults, disabled students, immigrants, and students of varied sexual orientations.

Anne Pruitt, dean in residence at the Council of Graduate Schools, has developed a sophisticated model that is intended to assist graduate

schools in recruiting students from under-represented groups and to prepare them for faculty and staff positions. Graduate programs, such as those
at the University of Maryland-College Park, Teachers College-Columbia
University, and California State University-Long Beach, have been successful in attracting and retaining students of color but much more needs
to be done, particularly as whites become a minority population in the
schools of many states. Senior student affairs officers (SSAOs) at both
two- and four-year institutions can help by identifying undergraduate student leaders who have potential for success in the field and recommending
them for graduate school. Programs can look for possible graduate students in successful peer academic advisement programs, such as the one at
Cerritos College in California; these students may not be aware of student
affairs graduate programs, which have been called by some "invisible graduate programs."

THE ROLE OF GRADUATE PROGRAMS IN CONTINUING
AND PROFESSIONAL EDUCATION

The third role for graduate faculty is that of providing professional development for currently employed or underemployed staff members at community colleges and for members of the community who might want to be
employed by a community college. Many community college presidents
are hiring high school teachers who are good teachers but who know little
about the specific needs of adult students. Graduate programs might use
models like the one developed by Tom Leemon in establishing the College
Teaching and Adult Learning (CTAL) doctoral program at Teachers College-Columbia University. To recruit strongly motivated students, Leemon
surveyed community college catalogs in the New York region, writing letters to invite faculty and staff members without doctorates to learn more
about the new doctoral program. Graduate classes, offered on weekends
and evenings, allowed faculty and staff members to experience professional renewal and to learn and apply new adult learning theories in the
projects they were required to institute, benefiting their students and their
institutions.

    A second alternative, currently being tried at California State Uni-
versity-Long Beach, involves adding two or three courses on community
colleges to the existing master's curriculum for Student Development in
Higher Education. These courses, offered in modules through the Continuing Education division, are available to student affairs master's students,
graduate students in such disciplines as science, math, and writing, current

community college personnel, and community members who are interested in working at a community college. The curriculum, developed by faculty members of the graduate program, along with the chancellor, president, and dean of a local community college, focuses on teaching in and administration of community colleges. The courses are taught by the president and chancellor at remote sites, using the latest technology, and the students receive supervised classroom and campus experience.

The role of graduate programs in renewing the knowledge base and skills of current employees is less clear. In the Computer Interactive Simulation Project, a NASPA project currently in its formative stages, graduate faculty members and SSAOs would design interactive learning modules for staff members at every levels — entry, mid-level, and senior — on the critical issues facing the profession, and these simulation programs could be used to provide on-site staff training on a continuing basis.

At a time of unprecedented change, both two- and four-year colleges must be concerned about planning for the next generation of staff members and updating the skills of those currently employed. The student affairs field must show professional leadership in instituting quality standards and encouraging continuing education if it is to remain a viable profession. Employees at both two- and four-year schools who completed their graduate education 20 years ago must learn about current learning theories, approaches to identity development, and modern technology. To accomplish this, mandated hours of continuing education and certification or recertification programs have been suggested, and graduate programs must work with professional associations and others to design and implement continuing education programs that will disseminate current research and knowledge. In 1999, the ACPA Senior Scholar/Fetzer project will distribute a white paper proposing an agenda for future research and for the new professional skills that will be needed by student affairs practitioners in the year 2000 and beyond.

THE ROLES OF STUDENT AFFAIRS PROFESSIONAL ASSOCIATIONS AND COMMUNITY COLLEGES

Professional associations have an obligation to provide leadership to ensure that there are enough well-prepared applicants who can assume community college and four-year college positions in the future. Groups such as the Council for the Advancement of Standards (CAS), NASPA, Commission XII of ACPA, and AACC should help design model curricula and establish channels of more systematic communication between two- and four-year colleges. The Quality Enhancement Task Force of ACPA must continue to address professional standards and continuing education for the field as a whole. In addition, student affairs practitioners and their associations need to assume responsibility for attracting a more diverse applicant pool to graduate programs in the field. Many graduate faculty members have never taught in a community college and require help in identifying current challenges and emerging needs. Community college students affairs administrators can serve on advisory boards to graduate programs and encourage local colleges and universities to add to existing or create new preparation programs. In this way and others, community colleges and professional preparation programs can form important partnerships that will help ensure the profession's future.

NEXT STEPS

A dialogue must take place between two-year college administrators and the faculty members of graduate programs responsible for training student affairs practitioners; and more data have to be collected to determine the characteristics and knowledge-base that will be needed for student affairs practitioners of the future. Succession planning along with a vision of an ideal future of and mission for the community college should inform program design. Graduate student affairs faculty members must work to learn more about the special needs and demands of community college work and should think about the role that continuing education plays as a service to the profession. They should also be aware that, in the future, professional practice in colleges and universities will come to increasingly resemble practice in community colleges.

At the beginning of the 20th century, both the community college and the student affairs profession emerged to serve the social needs of an industrial economy. The 21st century, with an economy based on information and its technology, will offer new opportunities for higher education to prepare students for a society whose nature we are only beginning to glimpse. Currently, it is especially important that we learn from each other and take special care to design training programs for our future leaders.

Reference
California Post-Secondary Education Commission (1996). Shared Responsibility: Strategies to enhance quality and opportunity in California Higher Education. San Jose: California Higher Education Policy Center.

LESSONS LEARNED ALONG THE WAY:
Planning for New Technology

by Michael Rooney

*I*n the midst of fundamental institutional changes currently occurring in two-year colleges, many of our beliefs and practices are being significantly challenged. These changes include:

•facing increased pressures to be accountable, show results, prove effectiveness;

•having to do more with less because of flattening or declining budgets;

•feeling more pressure to act as partners in community enhancement and workforce development efforts;

•dealing with an impending tidal wave of staff retirements, particularly among the faculty;

•coping with an explosive expansion of advanced technologies, such as distance learning;

•adapting to the ever-changing nature of our students.

We need to understand what all of these things mean to community college students, many of whom commute from car to classroom to car, juggling three or four responsibilities at any given time, thus making it difficult for the faculty or staff to engage or involve them outside the classroom. Astin (1985) and Tinto (1993) stress the importance of students making a connection, academic or social, in or out of the classroom, with someone or something at the institution. And, while it is inside the classroom where students have most of their contact with staff members and where their academic performance is judged, connections that take place outside the classroom can influence a student's persistence, attainment, and success.

Technological innovations can have a profound impact on student involvement in college life, especially as more institutions change from being management oriented to being student oriented. Such transformations are occurring at many community colleges, and those at four-year institutions may want to observe the results. On the one hand, modern technology can facilitate student access to programs and services, and, when used skillfully, engage and involve them in the curriculum. On the other hand, if the technology is not integrated into a fully human environment, it can create a campus made up of isolated students.

To explore the impact of technological innovations on our colleges, the author visited six community colleges between July 1 and December 31, 1996, to look at, among other things:

- their current application of technology to programs and services;
- their future plans for the technological delivery of programs and services;
- their perceptions of the implications of advanced technology for professional and staff development and training;
- the staffing issues and trends that had been identified;
- the identified implications, if any, of technological innovation for students;
- their plans for addressing the costs associated with the use of modern technology.

Approximately one week was spent at each institution interviewing a wide array of faculty, clerical staff members, administrators, and students. Their openness, honesty, and helpfulness insured that a great deal was learned, much of which could not have been anticipated. From the interviews, seven themes emerged:

- The Big Picture;
- The Student;
- Instructional Leadership and Teaching Faculty;
- Student Support Services;
- Management;
- Staff Attitude;
- Access, Training, and Support.

LESSONS LEARNED ALONG THE WAY

The Big Picture

The most important difference noted was between colleges that appeared to have a sense of the fit that existed between their technological agenda and their institutional mission and those institutions that had no clear concept of how these fit together. In the former, the mission had been spelled out and appeared to be accepted by staff members; at such institutions, the mission was reconsidered from time to time, and the technology agenda was developed and implemented as part of a natural process. Although this mode of operation may seem to be the obvious course, a surprising number of institutions proceeded differently. The issue here is whether the institution's mission is driving its use of technology or whether the technology is driving the institution. An important hallmark of successful institutions is their willingness to critically analyze their systems, to be open to introspection and self-scrutiny. Some of this scrutiny takes the form of re-engineering business processes to determine which programs and services can be enhanced by the application of advanced technology and which cannot. Four critical questions need to be asked and answered as part of this process:

- Is there proof that a particular technology is appropriate?
- Is there proof that it is effective?
- Is the technology as, or more, effective than current alternatives?
- Does research show the effect of this technology on learning?

The Student

A central issue involves the ways colleges use technology to facilitate the vitally important connections that students have with the institution and each other. Ideally, technology should play a role in forging those crucial connections that ensure a higher probability for student success.

Among the questions that were asked during my visits were: Was careful thought and attention being given to how technology, specifically the computer, could facilitate the integration of students to the programs and services offered at the college? Was thought being given to how technology could connect students with other students, both inside and outside the classroom? Regrettably, even though everyone agreed that the use of technology to bolster student connections and involvement was important, and that these results would likely occur as long as the technology imperative was implemented in a focused and organized manner, such planning seemed rarely to occur. This is a fertile area for a potential intra-institutional partnerships between offices of academic affairs and student services and is likely to become a crucial issue for four-year institutions as their students more and more come to more resemble community college students and come to have similar need for establishing connections with the institution and each other.

Instructional Leadership and the Teaching Faculty

The third theme that emerged involved instructional leadership and the teaching faculty. In colleges that were moving forward with a technology agenda, the long-term commitment to that agenda came from the top — from the president, the vice president, or dean — and, just as important, the faculty leadership played a partnership role in the planning and implementation of the agenda

In those institutions where careful and collaborative planning was evident, the faculty were thinking through such questions as: What types of delivery modalities were appropriate for what kinds of students and at what point in their educational development? Even more important, they were establishing criteria for assessing both the appropriateness and effectiveness of the delivery systems. In short, the technology was rightly considered to be a tool, not a panacea.

The faculty in those institutions where technology was being wisely applied, or at least considered openly, were aware they were being called upon to change. They were grappling with the process of change, asking why they should undergo these changes, and determining what benefits the changes could have for them. In other words, the technology was not being imposed upon them; they were involved, as a group, and moving forward as a result.

Student Support Services

The fourth theme focuses on student support services. Successful innovation will require student services staff to expand their skills in order to act as a valuable partner in the technology initiative. First, they must be technologically proficient. They do not have to become "techies," but they must be comfortable with the technology and able to use it nimbly. Second, at least some in student services must become current in the latest learning theory and brain research. This rapidly expanding body of knowledge has immense implications for how people learn — and it will have an impact on how programs and services are to be delivered in the future, with or without technology. Third, skills relating to the assessment of student readiness for distance learning and service delivery must be sharpened. Currently, we are not doing a good job of determining who is and who is not a candidate for distance learning courses, programs, and services as they are currently configured. Fourth, student services departments need to play a major role in conducting both formative and summative evaluations of the effectiveness of distance learning programming. This can only be done where there is a sense of mutual respect and trust between student services staff members and the instructional faculty. As with the other themes, a major question is the role of student services. Are they included in the planning and implementation processes? Is their perspective on the student valued and taken into account?

Management

The fifth theme centers on the college management staff — those who supervise the implementation of institutional visions. As with the Big Picture theme, a congruence and consistency of vision and effort is necessary to make the new technology a core element of the institution. Management is absolutely critical for the long-term successful implementation of the institution's technology initiative. Institutions that offer their managers proper skill training, support, and essential technology gain a management staff that is capable, forward-looking, and not threatened by change. Such managers, in fact, see themselves as being part of the advances that are being made, as vital participants in realizing their institution's future. In short, they have a long-term commitment to technology and distance learning.

Staff Attitude

The sixth theme deals with clerical staff attitude. The differences between institutions was quite apparent when it came to staff perceptions of technology and distance delivery of programs and services. Where staff members were involved and informed, because of strong college leadership and an effective infrastructure of support, they were fully behind the program. The level of such support plays a key role in determining whether staff members feel engaged or disenfranchised.

One staff member summed up the disillusionment that can result from inadequate support. She and her colleagues had been told that the new technology would free them from more mundane activity, so they would have greater responsibilities in their work with students. Because there was not an adequate level of training and technical support, the staff members would have to troubleshoot and attempt to fix the system every time there was a hardware or software failure, resulting in their having to do more work that was at a lower-level than had been the case before the implementation of the new technology. She was convinced that the introduced technology resulted in students being provided a *lower* level of service.

This may not be a fault of the new technology itself, but it certainly points to a problem in the planning and implementation of the system. Inadequately trained employees question the commitment of the college's leadership and become cynical about technology. Even more troubling, in some colleges clerical staff members are not included in the planning process at all, so their concerns are never heard.

Access, Training, and Support

The seventh and last theme is one of access, training, and support. In many ways, this provides the litmus test for the commitment of the institution to its agenda of technology and distance learning. A key question is what access to technology means. It should not mean merely providing employees or students with a desktop or laptop computer loaded with the newest software but must include providing adequate training and technical support.

The issue of haves and have nots, both among employees and students, must be addressed. Clearly, the inequity between students who have ready access to technology and those who do not cannot be ignored; if it is, the gap that already exists will widen even further. The resolution of this currently unaddressed social problem will become more critical as two- and four-year colleges enroll ever more diverse student populations. If the new technology is to be truly student centered, all students must have access to and opportunity to benefit from it.

BUILDING A PRINCIPLED TECHNOLOGY AGENDA

Thomas Jefferson said: "In matters of style, swim with the current. In matters of principles, stand like a rock." Using and integrating new technology is not a matter of style; if these tasks are to be done and done well, with the best interests of students, faculty and staff members as their focus, they should be treated as matters of principle. Technology and distance learning are not ends in themselves but means to an end. They are tools, and if they are to be properly utilized, they must contribute to student learning, development, and success. The use of modern technology is inevitable, and it must form part of, but not be, the vision and mission of the institution. Technological advances will help transform higher education, but that does not mean we cannot direct its course. To know with any certainty what is and is not appropriate, and to give appropriate direction to the technology agenda, we must pay close attention to these four factors:

- *Research,* to determine:
  a) what are our needs;
  b) what hardware is needed to meet those needs;
  c) who else is using this hardware; ·
  d) what relational database issues should be considered; and
  e) whether students will like and use the system and find it user-friendly.

• *Planning,* to address issues such as:

a)   whether the components should be networked or stand alone;

b)   the kind of internally- and externally-based technical support that will be provided;

c)   the training issues, including those of time and cost, that need to be considered by the staff;

d)   the relational database issues, identified by research, that should be considered;

e)   the need for students to like the system and find it user-friendly.

• *Implementation,* to include concerns such as:

a)   the ease with which the system can be upgraded;

b)   the compatibility of the system with existing equipment; and

c)   the times and places at which students can use the system.

• *Evaluation,* to determine the effectiveness of distance learning and technology-enhanced instruction, programs, and services.

IMPLICATIONS FOR FOUR-YEAR INSTITUTIONS

A basic assumption underlying this monograph is that four-year institutions will, increasingly, come to resemble two-year institutions, indicating that this approach to technological innovation also has implications for four-year institutions:

• As more community college students enter four-year college and university campuses, traditional approaches for involving students in campus life and methods for delivering services to them may need to change. Four-year institutions must determine what role technology can play in that change.

• If technology is to be a means for both serving students and involving them in campus life, many four-year institutions will have to determine how to change from being management oriented to being student oriented.

• Colleges and universities with minimal experience with nontraditional students may be tempted simply to rely on technology to serve such students. Ways of ensuring that the human touch, person-to-person contact, remains, will have to be found.

• Whatever changes in technology are undertaken by four-year institutions, the themes and principles suggested earlier in this section should be considered.

CONCLUSION

Community college students are pragmatists, and they often behave like consumers in their relationship to the college. For those developing technology agendas for a two- or four-year colleges, it is important be mindful of this practical consumer orientation. Technology can deliver instruction and service to students, but it has to do so in ways that are worth the students' effort. Finally, as educators we must be agile enough to move with the technological current, while at the same time helping our institutions keep a clear eye on core principles.

References

Astin, A. W. (1985). *Achieving educational excellence.* San Francisco: Jossey-Bass.

Tinto, V. (1993). *Leaving college: Rethinking the causes and cures of student attrition.* Chicago: University of Chicago Press.

ORGANIZING FOR SUCCESS
Ten Essential Tools

by Marguerite M. Culp

*M*ost of the authors in this monograph discuss what colleges and universities can learn from their community college colleagues about meeting the needs of students from populations historically under-represented in higher education. The insights, information, observations, and advice offered from the edge of the wave demonstrate how student affairs practitioners in community colleges predicted college and community needs, developed programs and services to meet these needs, and created the foundation for higher education student affairs work in the 21st century.

This section describes tools that student affairs practitioners at all higher education levels must have to meet the needs of their students, their institution, and their community in the years to come. Many of the tools emerged in the last decade from successful community college student affairs programs. New ways of thinking about the student body, staff and program development initiatives, effective use of technology, and strategies to provide the profession with better prepared entry-level practitioners are examples of these tools.

Often undervalued but nevertheless essential tools are those related to organization and staffing, both of which are clearly linked to the survival of the student affairs profession and to the success of the students that the profession serves. Although there is little research data to support one organizational structure or staffing pattern over another in community college student affairs programs (Culp, 1995), there is much anecdotal data about what not to do when organizing student affairs and hiring staff members, and valuable lessons to be learned from the experiments community colleges conducted in both areas during their brief history.

THE NAME GAME

Names are important in the student affairs profession. Student affairs departments that changed their names frequently in the 1970s and 1980s without changing what they did were ridiculed by faculty who saw the name changes as superficial window dressing. The metamorphosis of student services into student development at hundreds of community colleges without alterations in personnel or programs exemplified this phenomenon as does today's trend toward substituting student success services for the old student development title. Student affairs practitioners are not the only staff members responsible for developing students, and they certainly do not shoulder all of the responsibility for making sure that students succeed in college.

Organizational Tool #1: Practitioners need to name their area wisely, selecting a title with historical value (Student Affairs), a title that reflects their mission (Student Services), or a title that describes their relationship to the rest of the institution (Teaching and Learning Support Center).

THE ORGANIZATIONAL CHART

In an ideal world, reporting structures are irrelevant, since focus and sense of purpose determine program effectiveness. In the less than ideal actual academic world, however, organizational charts are extremely important. Directors of financial aid who report to the vice president of finance receive very different marching orders from their peers who report to the vice president of student affairs. Directors of admissions who report to the vice president for marketing have different objectives than directors of admissions who report to either the senior student affairs officer or the senior academic officer. Counselors scattered across the campus who answer to academic department chairs function in very different ways from counselors who report to a director of counseling or a dean of students, even if those counselors are housed in academic departments rather than a central counseling center. When staff members who provide basic student services report to nonstudent affairs administrators, four things tend to happen: a) programs and services become fragmented; b) staff members lose their focus and sense of purpose; c) the institution devalues student affairs; and d) neither students nor faculty receive the services they need.

Organizational Tool #2: Staff members engaged in student affairs work must report to a senior student affairs officer whose academic credentials include a significant number of courses in student affairs and whose career path demonstrates significant operational involvement in student affairs programming.

THE ORGANIZATIONAL PHILOSOPHY

"Hire good people and get out of the way" summarizes the management style of many founding community college presidents. That philosophy may have worked when a new community college opened every week in this country and taxpayers were so excited about having a college in town that they never questioned what they were getting for their money, but it does not work any more. The view from the balcony *is* different from the view from the classroom, and administrators have a responsibility to share that view and keep the organization focused on the future.

Senior student affairs officers must work with their staffs to develop a mission statement that complements that of the institution, define operational and strategic goals related to the mission statement, develop outcome measures to evaluate goal achievement, and demonstrate the effectiveness of student affairs programs and services. In addition, senior student affairs officers must use goal setting and evaluation to help staff members grow professionally and in a direction that benefits the institution, constantly monitor program and staff effectiveness, and aggressively weed out weak programs and people.

Organizational Tool #3: Organizations must clearly communicate their mission, philosophy, goals, and outcome measures to the student affairs staff; provide the staff with the tools to reach these goals; evaluate program and staff effectiveness; and eliminate ineffective programs and people.

LEADERSHIP OR MANAGEMENT?

The textbook answer to this question is that senior student affairs officers must be leaders and managers. In the real world, colleges with senior student affairs officers who are leaders will consistently outperform colleges who rely on managers to keep their student affairs programs afloat. Leaders are essential to the future of student affairs on any campus, particularly a community college campus because success belongs to those who can see the future, communicate what they see to others, inspire staff members to translate that vision into action plans, build trust and create coalitions, and spread the word about the value of student affairs. These are higher order leadership skills. Without leadership, student affairs practitioners are doomed to working behind the curve, constantly playing catch-up, and living on the fringes of the campus community rather than at the center where they belong.

Organizational Tool #4: Senior student affairs officers, particularly those who earned the position because of their management abilities, must develop their leadership skills. To develop these skills, senior student affairs officers must venture out of education into the world of business and organizational development. They need to read organizational theory, subscribe to business journals, attend leadership conferences and training institutes designed for business and civic leaders *not* educators, and shadow their counterparts in the business world.

THE SENIOR STUDENT AFFAIRS OFFICER

During the 1980s, a major management disease swept through America's community colleges. Believing that managers could manage anything and leaders could lead anywhere, whether or not they had any formal training in the areas for which they were responsible, community college presidents asked hundreds of faculty members or administrators with absolutely no training in student affairs to become senior student affairs officers. The chemistry teacher who chaired the Southern Association Self-Study was rewarded by being named dean of students and the popular speech teacher was permitted to leave the classroom and move into administration. When deans of students retired, they were not replaced, and their areas of responsibility were moved under the dean of instruction. The result was predictable. Five years later, community college presidents were questioning the effectiveness of their student affairs programs, wondering why programs and practitioners were not keeping pace with college and community needs, and dealing with low staff morale. With the exception of the president, senior student affairs officers have the most challenging administrative position on campus, primarily because they have to change roles so often to do jobs that require them to understand everyone else's responsibilities as well as their own.

During a typical community college work day, senior student affairs officers deal with issues related to advising, admissions, assessment and testing, classroom management, counseling, financial aid, judicial affairs, multicultural affairs, services for students with disabilities, teaching and learning styles, and veterans affairs; prepare and respond to audit reports; participate in writing, reviewing, and evaluating grant proposals; and respond to requests for support from the senior academic officer, the senior finance officer, the president, and the community.

Organizational Tool #5: Senior student affairs officers must be professionals with either a degree or significant graduate level course work in student affairs who have perfected their skills by working in a variety of student affairs positions. At a minimum, these skills must include the ability to: a) allocate resources based on college and department goals; b) build teams and partnerships; c) champion student affairs; d) communicate in many ways with various internal and external customers; e) create a climate that values change; f) delegate; g) focus energies and forecast events; h) link staff members to one another and to the community; i) leverage relationships to create programs that benefit students; h) motivate people and monitor programs; j) take risks; k) translate learning into action; l) translate research into programs; m) understand and shape the organizational culture; and n) use student success as a yardstick to measure the effectiveness of people and programs (Culp, 1996).

HIGH TECH VS. HIGH TOUCH

Student affairs graduate courses coupled with hands-on field experiences provide student affairs administrators with a foundation, a place to begin; but the future of student affairs may very well depend upon the ability of these leaders to define technology's place in student affairs. In an initial burst of high tech enthusiasm in the 1980s, some community colleges replaced people with machines, doing a real disservice to students who needed hands-on services. Others dug in their heels, refused to examine technology's role in student affairs, and increased personnel costs to the point that presidents began to outsource basic student affairs functions. The solution, community colleges soon concluded, was to find the balance between high tech and high touch but, as Culp (1996) demonstrates, that is easier said than done. Strong organizational and people skills are only the beginning.

Organizational Tool #6: Student affairs organizations must conduct technology audits, develop technology plans, determine how to use technology to accomplish their mission, and create training programs to help staff members update their technology skills. Technology audits provide a clear picture of the technological health of student affairs; technology plans outline long-range goals and identify priorities; and training programs help staff members overcome their fear of technology. More important, though, the process of determining technology's role in student affairs leads to the understanding that technology is just a tool, that the decision to remain technologically illiterate is not an option, and that student affairs staffs must create programs that blend high tech and high touch to increase the likelihood that students will succeed in the classroom.

Staffing Student Affairs. Most students never meet the senior student affairs officer, and for them the president is just a picture in the student handbook. The impressions they have of student affairs and the institution are created by the practitioners with whom they interact on a day-to-day basis: recruiters, admissions officers, financial aid clerks, testing specialists, advisors, counselors, job placement specialists, and student activities staff members. In the 1970s, community colleges grew so quickly that new staff members were fortunate to receive a 15-minute introduction to the college before they went to work. In the 1980s, student affairs generalists were replaced with specialists in a variety of areas. In the 1990s, many presidents sought to reduce costs by leveling student affairs: mid-managers were eliminated, master's degree staff members were replaced by bachelor's degree staff members, and staff members with associate degrees took the place of those with four-year degrees. Based on their experiences in the 1970s, 1980s, and 1990s, community colleges learned that the long-term health of the organization depended on the ability of staff members to understand their role in the organization, possess up-to-date job skills, realize that education is a business, and feel valued. They also learned that you get what you pay for.

Organizational Tool #7: Student affairs leaders must work with their staff members to write an accurate job description for every position on the organizational chart, identify the essential functions of each position and the skills required to perform those functions, establish realistic educational requirements for each position, and sell those requirements to the college community. Since the student affairs staff deals with students who are reluctant to travel from building to building or from campus to campus to access services, leaders should consider hiring generalists whenever possible. When specialists are hired, they need to be specialists willing to be cross-trained to deliver more than one service.

Organizational Tool #8: Student affairs organizations must provide all new employees with a uniform orientation to the college, a mentor who can introduce them to and guide them through the organizational culture, accurate job descriptions, continuous feedback on their job performance, and ongoing opportunities to upgrade the skills.

Organizational Tool #9: Teach everyone that education is a business that depends upon students for its existence. Using Lorenzo's definitions, as outlined by O'Malley (1997), help the organization to distinguish between the student as customer, the student as client, and the student as learner. Provide front line staff members with customer service training. Help advising and financial aid staff members to refine their consulting skills. Encourage counseling staff members to increase their teaching skills, their classroom time, and their contact with faculty.

Organizational Tool #10: Student affairs leaders must identify and reward staff members at all levels, celebrate successes, and share these successes with the college community. Recognizing and rewarding success must be a continual process not a once-a-year event.

TOWARD THE FUTURE

Student affairs practitioners in higher education who hope to lead their institutions into the 21st century must use a variety of tools to design organizational structures that meet the needs of tomorrow's colleges, develop programs and services that identify and serve tomorrow's students, attract and train staffs that are proactive and productive, and create campus cultures that value and reward strong student affairs programs and the practitioners who provide them. The ten tools described in this section will help student affairs practitioners, wherever they work, to increase the chances that their institutions — and the students they serve — will succeed.

References

Culp, M. M. (1995). Organizing for student success. In S. R. Helfgot and M. M. Culp (Eds.). *Promoting student success in the community college* (pp. 33-44). San Francisco: Jossey-Bass.

Culp, M. M. (1996). High touch + high tech = student success. In A. J. Natonak and P. Williamson (Eds.). *Shaping the future of student services: High tech-high touch-high quality* (pp. 26-34). Iowa City: ACT Press.

O'Malley, S. (1997). Student services with a smile. *Community College Journal, 68*(3), 8-12.

STAFF DEVELOPMENT
What University Student Affairs Staff Members Can Learn from their Two Year College Colleagues

by Marie Nock

Staff development in community colleges is known by many names: program development; professional development; staff, program, and organizational development; the teaching/learning center; or training and development. Most often the populations served are the faculty and staff. In the best programs, the needs of all employee groups are addressed, and full-time and adjunct staff members enjoy access to a full range of personnel development opportunities.

Florida provided national leadership in the early 1970s for staff development initiatives after the Florida legislature required community colleges to allocate an amount equivalent to 2 percent of their previous year's operating budget to support personnel development activities. Other states with notable staff and program development initiatives include California, Kentucky, Texas, Kansas, and Illinois.

As the gap between student needs and institutional cultures widens, two- and four-year colleges must allocate adequate resources for and pay more attention to staff development. A staff development program provides a systematic way for colleges to provide for the training and development needs of various employee groups, either individually or collectively, and to help employees function more effectively on a day-to-day basis and acquire new skills for future assignments.

Although many organizational options exist, the two strategies that seem to work best in community colleges and that have the greatest potential to benefit colleges and universities are:

1. Establish a Learning Center or Staff Development Center, staffed by full-time administrators who have staff development as their sole responsibility. A college advisory committee links the center to the various employee groups and divisions or areas of the college. The center offers training programs throughout the year, using internal resources and external consultants; offers reimbursement for additional graduate work; and funds travel related to professional development. The budget for this program is a percentage, usually between 1.55 percent and 3 percent, of the overall operating budget of the college.

2. Provide a member of the college community with release time, usually 20 percent to 40 percent of their assigned work time, to serve as

staff development coordinator. Appoint or elect a staff development committee to identify the staff development needs of all segments of the college community, and design and implement programs to meet these needs. Establish staff development days during which faculty and staff members are free to take part in the activities planned by the staff development committee.

Whichever option is selected, community colleges have learned that successful staff development programs must have five ingredients:

• The program must be aligned with the institution's mission and goals, and must serve to better prepare employees to meet the goals.

• Program participants must be recognized and rewarded for completing staff development programs and using the knowledge gained to improve programs, services, and individual performance.

• Programs must be of high quality, address real needs, and prepare participants to function more effectively when they return to the classroom or their offices.

• The administration, the faculty, and the classified and support staffs must view the program as providing needed services.

• The college must hire committed staff members, provide them with an adequate budget, establish appropriate expectations and support, and set up the staff development program at a location that offers high visibility and easy access.

The student services staff has unique development needs, which can be identified through a variety of nationally-used or campus-specific instruments. Since the thesis of this monograph is that two- and four-year institutions will become more and more similar in the years to come, colleges and universities can jump-start staff development programs by building on the needs analysis surveys conducted at community colleges, which have identified the following major training requirements for student affairs staff members in the next decade.

Customer Service Skills: All student affairs staff members need to enhance their ability to provide helpful, timely services to students, faculty, and others in the college community, whether these customers come to the college or call on the telephone. Learning to deal with difficult people is part of this training, but the primary emphasis should be on quality service to internal and external customers.

Supervisory Skills: Effective supervision is too important to be left to chance. Without training in performance management, personnel policies and procedures, communication and team building, supervisors are often left to supervise as they see fit. This can be costly to the institution in terms of lost productivity, declining morale, and the time spent dealing with grievances and lawsuits.

Dealing with difference: America's multiculturalism is nowhere more apparent in higher education than in the community college. Some staff members need training to master the finer points of dealing with gender, ethnic, and cultural differences. By helping institutions create a climate where all students, staff, and faculty feel valued and by making it possible for managers to spend less time dealing with grievances and lawsuits, this training pays for itself many times over.

Teaching Skills: Often the Student Life Skills or College Success courses are the domain of the student affairs department. Staff members who teach these courses may need training in developing a syllabus, planning lessons, enhancing their instructional skills, evaluating students, responding to student learning styles, providing and receiving classroom feedback, or teaching the adult learner. Even veteran faculty members need workshops to maintain their edge in the classroom.

Orientation: The best time to structure expectations for new employees and to transmit institutional mission and values is when new staff members begin their employment. Orientation programs must consist of much more than providing a list of fringe benefits. Partnerships can be established between the human resources office and the student affairs office for the development of a stimulating orientation process for newly hired student affairs staff.

Technology Training: An institution's investment in technology is wasted without ongoing training and evaluation. The staff needs to learn how to use the software licensed by their institution, how to access mainframe data, use the e-mail system, access information through the Internet, develop web pages, and conduct web-based research. Staff development programs provide initial training, follow-up training, and ongoing training for student affairs staff members.

Grant Writing: Equipping an entire student affairs staff with grant writing skills provides a training opportunity that more than pays for itself. With budgets tightening each year, knowing how to locate sources of revenue is a critical survival skill for student affairs practitioners, one that a staff development office can help them acquire.

Professional Effectiveness: To be effective, student affairs staff members need training in the following areas: time management, presentation techniques, guidelines for conducting effective meetings, problem solving and decision making strategies, and conflict resolution techniques. Many staff development programs contract with the student affairs staff to provide workshops in these areas for faculty and staff members, thus creating a partnership that benefits both the student affairs department and the college as a whole.

Personal Effectiveness: An unhappy, stressed-out staff is an ineffective staff. Because community colleges have learned that employees and institutions benefit from personal effectiveness training in the areas of stress management, wellness, financial planning, and retirement planning, a percentage of their staff development resources is allocated to such functions. This benefits the institution through reduced health care claims, increased productivity, and the fiscal fitness of staff members.

Process Consultation and Facilitation: Because of the role that the student affairs department plays in many organizations, faculty and staff members assume that its professional employees are skilled consultants, mediators, and group facilitators. If practitioners do not have these skills, both they and the college lose important opportunities to create partnerships that benefit everyone. Once again, a staff development program that provides student affairs practitioners with opportunities to develop their consulting, mediating, or group facilitating skills enhances the ability of the institution to respond to faculty and student needs.

Being an Agent of Change: With appropriate skills, student affairs administrators have the potential to be effective internal agents of change. To fulfill this role, they need to develop abilities in strategic planning, operational planning, re-engineering, managing internal changes, and delineating institutional visions.

Historically, universities have seen staff development in terms of travel to conferences or seminars. This perspective addresses some staff development requirements, but it does not offer a systematic way of addressing them or a cost-effective approach to changing the institution. Colleges and universities would do well to follow the lead of community colleges and create strong staff development programs that can bridge the gaps that exist between what is and what is needed, and provide faculty and staff members with tools they will need in the future. The wave of the future in staff development includes developing consortia of two-and four-year institutions to design and deliver integrated staff development programs, sophisticated teleconferencing resources, and web based in-service training opportunities, in addition to the programs and services currently offered.

Whatever approach is taken, colleges and universities need to understand that staff development programs have helped community colleges retain their competitive edge for over 20 years and have the potential to provide a similar service in colleges and universities.

RE-ENVISIONING PARTNERSHIPS
Practitioners' Views

by Erlinda J. Martinez and Bill Scroggins

*T*hroughout this monograph, the theme of partnerships, both within and outside the institution, appears repeatedly. The importance of partnerships to student success is emphasized as is a need to re-envision the student body. We agree that partnerships are essential for the success of students in both two- and four-year institutions, and as we re-examine our perceptions of students, we must also re-envision the nature of the particular partnership, forged around the issue of student transfer, that exists between community colleges and senior institutions.

The transfer of students is a primary mission of community colleges, and as administrators we are familiar with the programs and mechanisms that support this function. A danger exists, however, that we will complacently follow familiar or traditional methods rather than challenge ourselves to be innovative, or that we will assume that student transfers will occur even in the absence of careful review and continued vigilance to assure that our programs remain up-to-date and responsive to students. Historically, the transfer function has been a given; our roles and responsibilities as student services administrators are not. The challenges currently facing higher education, including many described elsewhere in this monograph, are such that we must move beyond tradition and think innovatively.

BEING STUDENT CENTERED

We must examine our colleges to see if our operations are student centered by, for example, reviewing the paperwork required for transferring students. If we believe that we are serving the student and have as our goal his or her transfer, we should avoid requiring the student to complete duplicate forms or to provide identical information to both the community college and the four-year institution. We must consider not only forwarding transcripts electronically, which is common, but also using computers to process the entire package of forms and paperwork. Technology can be used to support students, but only if good and accurate information is available to them.

If the student is the center of our interest, then as many transfer options as possible should be made available. Rather than merely bringing representatives of state and other local institutions to the campus, the office responsible for transfers should also invite representatives of religious, ethnic, and private institutions to meet their students. Community college students are busy with family, work, and other responsibilities, so the transfer process must be as undemanding of time and in-person trips to the campus as possible. Transfer-oriented services should be offered on weekends and at remote sites. While many of us at community colleges adjusted to the needs of our students long ago, many faculty and staff members at four-year schools have not, and may be unwilling to acknowledge the necessity of such adjustments, making collaboration with them difficult. Seamless transfer does not exist for students whose lives are fragmented and, consequently, we must pay close attention to the processes, information, and methods that support their efforts to move on.

Curriculum and Articulation

The transfer function in two-year institutions is premised on the assumption that the community college provides the first two years of postsecondary education and the baccalaureate-granting institution the final two years. The first two years involve major preparation, both general education (GE) and elective courses, with articulation agreements that reflect these categories, specifying whether a particular course can be applied to a major, a general education requirement, or is transferable only as an elective. Sometimes, however, statewide inter-system and local inter-institution articulation processes use different categories causing confusion for students.

The California State University (CSU) has specific general education requirements, and individual community colleges submit courses annually to be evaluated by a joint group of CSU and California Community College (CCC) faculty. A separate set of Intersegmental General Education Transfer Curriculum (IGETC) requirements has been developed which meet both University of California (UC) and CSU requirements. While the same joint group of CSU and CCC faculty members evaluate courses for IGETC, UC faculty members review these courses on their own. Each of the UC campuses has its own GE requirements for the majors they offer, and community colleges may articulate GE courses on a campus-to-campus basis. The CSU and CCC faculty support a California Articulation Number (CAN) system which establishes a course as acceptable for major preparation at any of the 23 CSU campuses if any four of them have articulated that course. Individual community colleges may establish major preparation agreements with particular four-year campuses, but there is no statewide system for acknowledging full preparation for the major. CSU allows each CCC to certify courses for elective credit, but UC reviews each course individually. If all this appears convoluted, imagine how it must appear to the students who are trying to move through the process. Further, imagine how ludicrous we would seem were we to assert that the CCCs, the CSUs, and the UCs were partners in the articulation process.

The traditional process of articulation must be rethought. Two things are clear. First, the present process is driven by the overriding concern of four-year institutions to protect what they see as the integrity of the baccalaureate degree. Second, in many cases the current process is confusing to students and requires them to repeat courses or take additional courses when they change their transfer goals or are redirected upon transfer. No one will argue with the fact that the baccalaureate degree must be strong and relevant, but there is a compelling public interest in assuring that the scarce resources devoted to higher education be used efficiently. When students must retake courses upon transfer because of poor or absent articulation agreements or, even worse, because of the play of institutional egos, the public interest is not served. When the lack of uniform requirements among receiving institutions results in students having to delay upper division work until courses required by a particular four-year college are completed, time to degree is unnecessarily extended. Common course numbering systems may help in some states, as can guarantees of transferability. As long as individual universities can decide to accept or not accept a course or group of courses, however, students will continue to pay a price that they need not, and should not, pay.

The authority structure for articulation is upside down. Although community colleges educate the majority of lower division students in many states, and thus have the greatest experience with the curricula and the needs of the students, they and their students are held hostage to university requirements. It is possible for us to protect the integrity of the baccalaureate degree and provide smooth transfer, but collaboration requires partners who are on equal footing. Where the above barriers exist in current articulation structures, we can rewrite them using these two principles:

- The content and standards for lower division major preparation, general education, and elective credit are to be mutually agreed upon by faculty at community colleges and four-year institutions.
- The faculty at community colleges should have the power to certify that their courses cover the required content and meet established standards, with four-year faculty participating in regular program review.

The institutions of each state would be united in letting students know that a given set of courses would be sufficient for transfer from any community college to any public baccalaureate-granting institution in the state, even though the specific courses might vary from college to college. This would represent real collaboration and a real partnership.

Four-year schools with unique programs could express that uniqueness in the upper division curriculum, as is done in the transition to graduate school. Each graduate school has particular strengths, but all uniformly accept baccalaureate preparation from accredited institutions. They do discriminate, accepting all of the credits of some degrees, some of the credits of others, and none of the credits of still others. Opportunities should exist for two- and four-year college faculty in each of the two or three dozen common transfer majors to meet jointly and develop content and standards. A concomitant requirement to assure quality should involve a strong system of program review at each community college, enforced through both accreditation and continued involvement in the review process by four-year faculty members in specific disciplines. This is similar to the way many community colleges use advisory committees in career programs.

Beyond streamlining articulation, other cooperative ventures should be encouraged. Joint admission programs give qualified students the opportunity to acquire their first two years of education at a community college without giving up their eligibility at the university. Cross-enrollment agreements allow students flexibility in scheduling while reducing fees for duplicate services. Use of university mentors in specific subject areas for community college students would increase learning for both participants. Internship programs which place professionals in training on community college campuses provide valuable hands-on experience for the interns and much needed assistance for the community colleges. Faculty exchange programs broaden experiences and cross-fertilize curricula. These joint ventures increase dialogue about our shared curricula and, increasingly, our shared students, and they provide informal as well as formal sites where ideas can be exchanged and relationships developed.

Student Services and Activities

Many community colleges have programs that assist high school students in their transition to the community college, such as summer bridge-type programs, early start programs, and honors programs for high school students. Collaboration with four-year institutions to support student transition is not as common. We also have experience with the reverse transfer student, who may begin at the university and then, for any number of reasons, choose to transfer to the community college. When approaching four-year institutions about shared services, the fact that those services are directed to a shared student body, which often moves back and forth between institutions, must be stressed. Whether the shared service involves developing an education plan or providing career guidance, the student is the beneficiary of service articulation between the community college and the four-year institution.

The concept of a shared student body provides an avenue through which we can rethink the areas where collaboration would benefit students. Two- and four-year institutions in the same urban area, for example, might share bus and transportation services and even residence halls. Connections can be established through clubs and other organizations; for example, ethnic clubs on both campuses would benefit from shared activities. Such combined events not only bring students together but support transfer. There might well be a target audience that would especially benefit from close collaboration, such as international students or re-entry students. It is not unusual to have student services designed especially for athletes, who are required to meet academic progress requirements to maintain eligibility. Quite often an athlete will know exactly what is required to transfer and has been advised how to do it. Unfortunately, an English major may not have been given the same clear direction. Closely supported and collaborative programs like athletics show the value of this approach for all students in all majors.

Some services can be shared through technology. For example, we can use computers to analyze transcripts sent from one college to another or certify the completion of general education requirements. This requires a standardization of electronic exchange programs and a significant collaboration between both the admissions and records offices and computer center personnel. This may sound elementary, but as student services administrators we need to work with our colleagues in computer services and at four-year schools to keep up to date with technological advances and to explore the use of shared systems. We cannot accept traditional methods based on long held assumptions or because staff members are resistant to change.

Facilities and Business Services

Many community colleges and four-year institutions share facilities, but even in this area more agreements should be explored. In addition, we can consider the economies of scale that come from the joint purchasing of supplies or computer equipment. For certain projects, even the sharing of heavy equipment is possible. When natural disasters such as floods, hurricanes, and earthquakes occur, mutual aid agreements may be useful. As we merge facilities and business services, costs are reduced and the ties between community colleges and four-year institutions are strengthened, while services to students are enhanced.

Marketing

Resources for student services continue to be tight in many two- and four-year institutions. As student services administrators, we are continually called upon to justify even the smallest portion of the college budget we receive. Collaboration between two- and four-year schools can be used to stretch those dollars while not just maintaining, but actually improving, the quality and relevance of services.

Several audiences need to hear this message. First, the state legislature appropriates both general funds and those targeted for special projects. Local representatives must be convinced that both the two- and four-year schools in their districts will benefit from funds allocated to shared services. In some states, legislative changes might be necessary to remove statutory barriers to shared facilities or resources. Colleagues at neighboring colleges and universities also may need to be persuaded of the possibilities opened up by joint ventures. Personnel already associated with both institutions and successful collaborations already in place can be used as bridges that can increase cooperation between institutions. Bringing together regional senior student service officers at two- and four-year institutions for brainstorming sessions would provide benefits for everyone.

Look at your own operation. Identify those areas where transition services benefit students and those areas that confuse or hinder students in the transfer process. Build an action plan that addresses these concerns through collaborative efforts. Estimate how joint ventures can save your district money or can allow your institution to gain access to previously unavailable funds. Use concrete examples of shared programs that work, including before-and-after cost and effectiveness evaluations. Then, take your action plan through your institution's decision making process.

SUMMARY

For too long, higher education has treated the transfer function as if its value to students would provide sufficient impetus for students to undergo the process, no matter how many barriers. The chasm between two- and four-year colleges has been bridged by the thinnest of fibers. The needs of students must be considered and student services administrators are best positioned to institute needed changes. Transfer information must be readily available to students; the steps of the transfer process must involve minimum duplication and maximum collaboration; articulation must not be hampered by academic turf battles and must be based on aligned curricula instituted by faculty members who see each other as equals; services for what is, essentially, the same student body at two- and four-year schools should be shared and coordinated; partnerships that involve shared facilities and pooled business activities should be encouraged.

It is a given that transfer requires participation by both community colleges and four-year institutions. Collaboration, especially in some of the areas that have been suggested here, is not. Higher education institutions pay lip service to transfer as a central mission, but their actions often belie their words. Our institutions must be called to task. Student services administrators need to review programs that are in place, moving beyond our historical role and traditional methods of doing business. We owe it to our students to think in new ways and to embrace change in order to maintain vibrant community colleges and healthy colleges and universities that better serve students and meet their needs.

About the Authors

MARGUERITE M. CULP recently joined the staff of Austin Community College in Austin, Texas, as associate vice president for retention and student services. She previously served as dean of students at Seminole Community College in Sanford, Florida.

STEVEN R. HELFGOT is director of community relations and professor of counseling at Cerritos College in Norwalk, California.

JACK BECHERER serves as vice president for student development at Moraine Valley Community College in Palos Hills, Illinois.

JANNA HOEKSTRA BECHERER is a counselor at South Suburban College in South Holland, Illinois.

CYNTHIA S. JOHNSON directs the Master's Degree Program in College Student Development at California State College-Long Beach where she also serves as professor of educational psychology and administration.

ERLINDA J. MARTINEZ is vice president for student development at Cerritos College in Norwalk, California.

MARIE NOCK has been involved in training and development in both the public and private sectors for over 20 years. She currently serves as director of planning, operations and technology in the College Training and Development Office at Miami-Dade Community College in Miami, Florida.

LINDA REISSER recently collaborated with Arthur Chickering to update *Education and Identity*. She serves as dean of students at Suffolk County Community College's Ammerman Campus.

MICHAEL ROONEY is district director of student development for the Maricopa Community Colleges in Tempe, Arizona.

BILL SCROGGINS serves as president of the state-wide faculty senate for the California Community College System. He is also a professor of chemistry at Chabot College in Haywood, California.